UP CLOSE

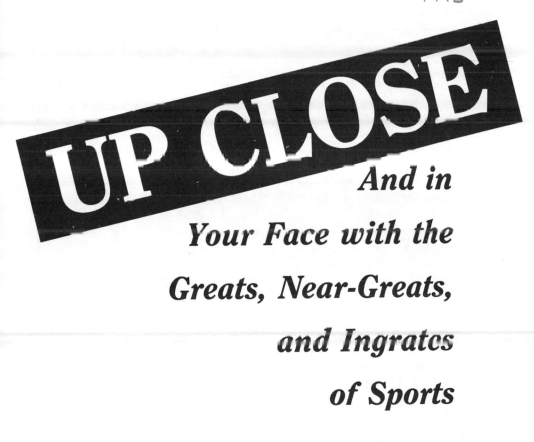

UP CLOSE

And in

Your Face with the

Greats, Near-Greats,

and Ingrates

of Sports

Roy Firestone
with Scott Ostler

HYPERION

NEW YORK

The author gratefully acknowledges permission from ESPN for use of the title, and for permission to publish interviews from *Up Close*.

Library of Congress Cataloging-in-Publication Data

Firestone, Roy.
    Up close : and in your face with the greats, near-greats, and ingrates of sports / Roy Firestone with Scott Ostler. – 1st ed.
        p.   cm.
    ISBN 1-56282-869-X
    1. Sports–United States–Anecdotes.   2. Athletes–United States–Anecdotes.   I. Ostler, Scott.   II. Title.
GV583.F56 1993
796′.0973–dc20   93-16221
                                                                       CIP

First Edition
10 9 8 7 6 5 4 3 2 1

Contents

Foreword

Just as Alabama has always taken great succor that no matter how bad off it may be, it always can count on Mississippi to bring up the rear, so us sportswriters have viewed sportscasters. However maligned we might be by the general populace or by the sweaty heroes we write about, we have known in our hearts that still were we noble reporters! Yeomen professionals! Citadels of integrity! And, above all: better than sport*scasters!*

Sure, sportscasters might make more money, but they were merely glib and corrupt, golden throats who wouldn't know the truth and/or journalism if it batted cleanup. Almost half a century ago, Jimmy Cannon, who was candid enough to label his own newspaper sports department "the toy department," baldly declared: "With few exceptions, sports broadcasters function as publicity men, not reporters."

Amend this slightly, change the adjective "few" to, say, "some"—and that's about all that perception has changed with time. Or, as the (slightly) dirty joke has it, the woman goes to the marriage counselor . . . again. "What's the problem this time?" he inquires.

"Well," she replies, "if you recall, my first husband was a

preacher, and he wouldn't, and my second husband was a drunk, and he couldn't, and now my third is a sportscaster"—

"And?"

—"and he just sits on the end of the bed and tells me how great it's going to be."

But, even if we sportswriters don't like to admit it, sportscasters are not just facile entertainers anymore. There are today before the microphones many more men (and even a few women) who are every bit as honest and informed—and, yes, even literate—as we sportswriters decide that we are by the time we close the bar each night. And Roy Firestone takes his own best colleagues one better, too. He is every bit an original at what he does, and yet to describe this rare talent it is really best to use an old-fashioned word: interlocutor. Roy Firestone doesn't *cast* anything. He talks. He discusses. He parleys. He converses directly with people in sport in an intelligent way that not only engages us as eavesdroppers but reveals the guests to us.

This is not as easy as it may seem, either, for few athletes are naturally well-spoken, and since the ones that matter the most make unholy sums of money nowadays, they are not necessarily inclined to favor us in the press with their wisdom. Why should they bother talking? Times have changed since Dizzy Dean allowed: "A lot of the folks that ain't saying ain't, ain't eating." The fellas in sport these days ain't saying much, and it ain't hurting them a tall.

But Roy knows how to bring people out, how not only to make them speak to him, but to enjoy doing it. This is his real magic, the ability to encourage people in sport to participate willingly—even with enthusiasm—in civil, coherent English conversation. When he is done with his guests, out of the raw material of simple conversation he has usually constructed a finished human product that we understand much better. Roy's dialogues enhance our appreciation of the people in sport, and they invest his profession with a wit and grace we have not seen anywhere else—not even with sportswriters.

—Frank Deford

Introduction

What follows on these pages has little to do with the ills of sport—the greedy owners, egocentric athletes, distorted values, preoccupation with money.

This is a book about something I love—my job. I'm living out my childhood fantasies, and I offer no apologies.

For the last thirteen years, as host of *SportsLook* and now *Up Close* on ESPN, I have been fascinated, repulsed, amused, horrified, threatened, delighted, enlightened, and exhilarated. I confess that I have not been bored.

My guests are a unique subculture of humanity—people who are gifted, often spiritual, sometimes articulate, almost always entertaining.

They have in common the quest for victory, the pursuit and realization of dreams played out in public under the harsh spotlight of sports that exposes the best and the worst.

When the show is good, it usually has to do with giving. My favorite programs have been with people who are open, willing, reflective, at ease with who and what they are and give of themselves to their viewers.

Not all are great thinkers, which is good because, God knows, neither am I. But they each have something great to share—insights, humor, glimpses of character.

It is, for me, an ongoing education. I am majoring in people, and every interview is a new course.

Many people think I have a great job. They're right. If it ended tomorrow, after nearly four thousand shows, I would treasure the experience and know that I'm infinitely better off for having had it.

Some critics have said I'm too soft on my guests, and they may be right. I purposely avoid the style of assailing, humiliating, or attacking a guest. A guest on my show is like a guest in my home. I think I'm a good listener, and my instincts are less toward finding their warts and blemishes, more toward finding their inner workings—who they are, and why. That's what got me interested in sports in the first place, and it's what continues to fascinate me.

Besides—it's my show.

Another criticism, to which I plead guilty, is that we've had too few women guests. I could explain that sports is male dominated, but in truth, I've got to try harder. (And so do the women, especially the tennis players—Monica Seles canceled five times, and Martina Navratilova twice.)

I've been fortunate to have been associated with what I'm positive are some of the most talented, loyal, committed, and hard-working people in the TV business. In any business.

I would like to thank, in no particular order: Bob Seizer, Josh Kaplan, Jason Schirn, Cindy Katz, John Carlin (who labored like a monk transcribing interviews for this book), Tom Weber, Harold Reiser, Chris Stegner, Richard Coniglio, Leslie Wells, and the late Ray Hughes. I owe them more than thanks, I owe them my career.

Also, my thanks to the people who believed in me way back in the old days, and to those at ESPN—Steve Bornstein, Loren Matthews and Steve Anderson.

I dedicate this book to my father, who taught me how to love sports; my mother, who taught me how to love life; my wife, Midori; and my boys, Andrew and Nicholas. I am a product of your sacrifices and your caring. I hope I have done you proud.

—Roy Firestone
December 1992

ONE

BATBOY

It all started in the clubhouse of the Baltimore Orioles
That was the birthplace of my show business career. You hear
entertainers talk about paying their dues by performing in seedy
strip joints, but how many of them ever worked a room where the
audience was getting undressed?

It was an unconventional way to launch a career, but then, my
career is unconventional. I have hosted a TV sports interview
show since 1980, and my nightclub act keeps me on the road
about one hundred nights a year.

I couldn't have done it without the Orioles.

Growing up in Miami, Florida, I loved sports. The physical battle
was interesting, but what I was really drawn to was the drama, the
spectacle, the theater of the games.

I was not a batting-average memorizer. I loved the color of the
grass at old Miami Stadium, the light and shadows across the field
in late afternoon, the smell of cigars in the stands, and the clatter
of the spikes on the concrete walkway between the dugout and
the clubhouse.

I collected photos of dramatic and colorful sports moments, and
affiliated myself with the teams that had the coolest uniforms. By

the fourth grade, I was an avid collector of caps, shirts, and other sports memorabilia, with never a thought of selling or trading the stuff.

The Baltimore Orioles were my team. They not only had great uniforms, but Miami was their spring training home. We were probably bigger Orioles fans than the people living in Baltimore, because we Miamians packed all of our emotional fandom into those two months each spring. The start of spring training was like the circus coming to town, the most exciting time of the year.

My father, Bernard, who has a notions business in Miami, often took my brother Glenn and me to spring games at Miami Stadium. We would sit in the distant reaches of the ballpark. I loved it, but I kept thinking there must be some way to get closer to the players than this. I could join the group of kids sticking programs through a fence and begging for autographs, but that wasn't good enough. By the sixth grade, I'd hit upon a scheme, but I didn't get the nerve to try it until I was a junior in high school in 1970.

My thinking was this: the Orioles probably didn't bring their regular batboys to spring training. That would be too expensive, and those batboys were probably still in school. The Orioles must hire Miami kids to help around the clubhouse and with the bats. Why not me?

Incidentally, my plan had absolutely nothing to do with vowing to be a great batboy, to work harder than the other guys and really impress people with my hustle. All I wanted was a way to get closer to the players.

In mid-February I phoned the local newspaper and asked when the Orioles' equipment truck was due in town. I was referred to Miami Stadium, and after some persistent phone work, I finally was connected to someone who seemed to know when the truck would arrive.

"Why do you want to know, kid? The ballclub doesn't work out until a week later."

"I don't care about the players," I said. "I just want to help unload the gear."

The guy probably thought I was weird, but he said, "They'll get here about noon next Wednesday."

Early Wednesday morning I had my mom drive me to the

stadium. I told her I was going to meet the players, get some autographs. She waited a while with me, then had to leave.

When my father tells this story now, he talks about how "Roy had an opportunity to interview for the Orioles' batboy job." Well, this is how the "interview" went:

I took up a position near the clubhouse door, sat on the ground and waited. Noon came, no truck. The day wore on. The stadium is in a bad part of town, and it was hot, and I was getting discouraged. There wasn't another living soul in sight, until a pitiful, mangy, three-legged dog hopped down the street and sat down to wait with me. The whole scene was like something out of a David Lynch movie.

Finally, about three o'clock, a huge moving van pulled up, with BALTIMORE ORIOLES and the cartoon bird painted on the side. The driver, an old man, got out and started to unload the stuff. He was alone. I asked if I could help.

"Get the hell out of here, kid," he barked.

That was the start of my job interview. This guy was nicer to the three-legged dog, whose name was Little Bit and who turned out to be the Orioles' clubhouse mascot.

I hung around. The old man was taking all the stuff into the clubhouse through a swinging door. He couldn't figure a way to prop it open, so I said, "Can I hold the door for you?"

"Yeah, okay."

Man! It was unreal. He was pushing in racks of uniforms. There's Number 5—Brooks Robinson! Number 26—Boog Powell! All the hats and bats, it was just too cool.

I started to worm my way in.

"Can I help you with the bats? . . . Want me to give you a hand with those boxes?"

Finally I wore the guy down and joined the unloading, pausing frequently to admire the goods.

"Wow, this is Boog's bat."

"Gimmie that thing, kid!"

When we finished, I told the old man that I'd love to come back again and work in the clubhouse.

"We have our own clubhouse boy," he said.

"I'd just like to be an addition," I told him.

Apparently I didn't look like a terrorist. He grumbled that I could come back the following Saturday, shine some shoes, help with some clean-up, he'd see how I did.

Come Saturday, the old man, whose name was Izzy, gave me an old, baggy, rumpled, flannel Orioles uniform, so I wouldn't get shoe polish on my own clothes. There was a "B" game that afternoon, and they didn't have a batboy, so I volunteered, and instantly became the Orioles' spring batboy.

I was in the door for my first intoxicating taste of bigtime sports and showbiz.

As I said before, my master plan called for a minimum of work and a maximum of gawking at and hanging around with the players. In order to do that, I had to be more than just a batboy and shoe-shiner. So I broke out the comedy.

As early as I can remember, I always did impressions around the house, of people on TV and in the news, friends, and family. Not long before the batboy gig came about, I had launched, in a very elementary way, my showbiz career.

Miami back then was the world's mecca for Borscht Belt–type comedians. Every hotel and old folks' home in Miami, all several thousand of them, had nightly entertainment. I talked myself onto the bill at a few of the clubs, doing my impressions—Jack Benny, Hubert Humphrey, Jimmy Stewart, Ed Sullivan, the old standards. I never even told my parents what I was up to, because I knew I wasn't very good and I didn't want to embarrass them.

The audiences were mostly very old people. One place I worked, the people in the audience had wooden clackers, which dated back to vaudeville days. Instead of laughing or applauding, they would clack their clackers. Very strange.

Now, suddenly, I had a new, hipper audience—a major league baseball team. My first day on the job, I started goofing around in the clubhouse, doing some of my impressions. Earl Weaver, the manager, and a couple of players laughed at me, probably more out of disbelief than anything. One of them told me, "Why don't you get up in front of all the guys and do some of this before we go out on the field?"

Why not? My second day as batboy, I stood in the middle of the splintered wooden floor of the clubhouse and entertained the Orioles. They laughed at this nerdy kid wearing glasses and a baggy uniform, doing impressions and jokes.

About an hour after my very first performance, Ralph Salvon, the Orioles' portly trainer, walked up to me on the field.

"Say, are you Roy Firestone, the kid that was just doin' those impressions?"

"Yes," I said, proudly.

"You were just up there, entertainin' the whole club?"

"Yes."

"And you're our new batboy?"

"Yes I am," I said, feeling very cool.

Ralph started yelling.

"Who the hell do you think you are?! Get the hell back in there and get to work!"

But there was no stopping me. My act became part of the players' daily routine: saunter into clubhouse, eat donuts, sip coffee, read mail, play cards, oil the glove, put on the uniform, catch the comedy stylings of batboy Roy, play ball.

Athletes, I believe, appreciate anyone who's got enough guts to put himself on the line in front of an audience, because it's what they do every day. And guts I had. Material, I was a little light on. I had maybe five minutes of schtick, which I used up the first day. After that, I would wing it. Along with my stock impressions of Lyndon Johnson and Ed Sullivan, I'd do various Orioles. Earl Weaver was easy to do, so were Davey May and Curt Motton, and I got laughs putting a mop on my head and impersonating Frank Robinson, the chief justice of the Orioles' kangaroo court.

I did my act daily—in the clubhouse, around the batting cage, on bus rides. The Orioles even shared me with other teams. Paul Blair, the great center-fielder, would grab me during batting practice and march me over to some friend of his on the other team.

"You gotta do Ed Sullivan for this guy," Blair would tell me. Or, "Do your Davey May impression."

When the Braves came to Miami, Blair pointed out the Braves' manager, Lum Harris. I didn't know that Lum happens not to have the best sense of humor, and is every bit as exciting as his name.

"Why don't you go over and ask Lum if you can do your impressions for his team."

I sauntered over to Lum and said, "Mr. Harris, my name's Roy

Firestone, I'm the Orioles' batboy. I do some impressions, I'm kind of funny, and the Orioles want to know if it's okay if I entertain your guys before the game."

Lum stared at me as if I'd offered to set fire to his team's bat rack.

"You gotta be kiddin' me," he said. "Get the hell out of here."

Mostly, it was a glorious spring. The Miami *News* even did a feature story on the Orioles' comedian batboy.

I hadn't planned in advance to become a batboy comedian. There was a lot of ham in me, for sure, and I wanted some sort of recognition. Instead of, "Hey, kid, bring me another bat," it was, "Hey, Roy, come over here and do Earl."

The job was a thrill. I loved every second, even though the work itself was dirty and demeaning and the hours were long, with no days off. I reported to work at one o'clock in the afternoon for a 7:30 game and worked until at least one in the morning, shining shoes and sweeping. On the plus side, I retained my amateur standing, since the Orioles didn't pay me a dime in two springs. I should've had a better agent.

That didn't matter. I was wide-eyed and constantly amazed. If you're a starry-eyed fan, there really is nothing like the sights and sounds of a baseball clubhouse.

And the smells. There are three smells that are still vivid to me. Every morning they would hit me at once—the cigar smoke, mostly from the Cuban players, Mike Cuellar and Chico Salmon; the pine tar, which would get under my fingernails and into my skin and stay there for weeks; and Bazooka bubble gum, which was delivered by the truckload, like coal for a furnace.

It was a kick to walk in there every day and see my heroes— Boog, Frank Robinson, Brooks Robinson, Jim Palmer, Blair. I don't know what I first expected; I guess I thought they'd be as serious and poised as they had been when I watched them from the top row of the grandstand. Not so. It was like a group of kids with no supervisor. Guys walking around in their underwear, throwing things, playing practical jokes, cursing, razzing one another, nursing hangovers, goofing off.

I grew up worshiping Boog Powell. That first day on the job I had walked up and said, "Hi, Boog, I'm Roy Firestone, I'm the new batboy."

Here's a 250-pound man without a stitch of clothing, smoking a cigar, reading the newspaper. It was a strange scene.

Nobody seemed to mind that I was the worst batboy who ever lived, the very last kid you'd ever want to put in charge of organizing anything, like equipment or clothing. The players would always be yelling, "Hey, Roy, I got two left shoes here," or, "Where the hell's my batting glove, Roy?"

In my first week, Don Baylor and Don Buford called me over and asked me to get them some left-handed bats. I had played some baseball, Little League and sandlot, I knew there were no left-handed bats. Yet this was the big leagues. Apparently they had more sophisticated equipment. I panicked.

"They didn't tell me anything about left-handed bats," I stammered.

"Well, I'm a left-handed hitter," Buford said, "I can't bat with these."

"I can go look for 'em," I said.

"Ask Mr. Weaver where they are," they told me, directing me to the gruffest man in baseball.

Earl stroked his chin, said he wasn't sure where the lefty bats were. He directed me to another guy, who directed me to a coach, and so on. I was a human pinball. I spent half an hour chasing the left-handed bats before I caught on.

Field awareness was not my strong suit, either. My concentration would waver. Many times I grabbed a ball that was still in play. Sure, they were just exhibition games, but it was unnerving for the umpires and players when I would run out and snatch a wild pitch that had rolled to the backstop. I saw a ball in foul territory, I figured it was mine. Foul pop flies? I collided with three or four catchers. Thank God baseball blooper tapes hadn't been invented.

There is no place in the world like a baseball clubhouse. Where else can a guy feel right at home in a jockstrap and shower shoes, smoking a huge cigar, practicing his golf swing with a baseball bat?

The Mets once closed their clubhouse to the media before games, so they could concentrate on game preparation. A writer peeked in one night and saw Tom Seaver riding a tricycle. It's a strange world.

If the bomb is ever dropped and you're looking for shelter, try to find a baseball clubhouse. At least you won't starve. There is an endless supply of free food—donuts, soup and sandwiches, racks of candy and gum, boxes of chewing tobacco and snuff, ice cream, sodas, beer, barbecue chicken and ribs, pasta. Every day fans would send in loads of cookies and cakes and pies for their favorite players.

This is all in addition to the players' daily meal money. And you wonder why these guys have to be forced to retire.

I was awestruck by the sheer volume of equipment. One player might have forty-five bats, fifty pairs of baseball shoes, a dozen mitts, crammed in his locker. The players gave me whatever wore out or broke, so I was always watchful.

"Hey, Boog," I'd say, "that jersey is pretty worn out."

"Naw, Roy, it's fine."

"Really, it looks pretty shabby, you should have Clay get you a new one, throw that one out."

Clubhouse attendants and trainers, I would learn, are all characters, old and crusty, like refugees from a carnival. Their prevailing attitude is one of perpetual annoyance with the demands of the players.

Jim Bouton, in *Ball Four,* tells a typical clubbie story. He's with the Yankees and one of the players asks the clubbie if he can stock some grape soda in the pop cooler.

The clubbie gets a pained expression and says, "You guys, I know if I get this grape soda, you're just gonna drink it all."

One day I told the equipment man, Clay Reid, "Paul Blair needs some more bats, he's down to his last two."

Reid said, "Paul Blair? Screw Paul Blair. All he does is break his bats."

It was great to be a kid, a big fan, and suddenly be on the inside, the inner circle, get to know what the players are really like. This was not an ordinary team, of course. At least four of the guys were future Hall of Famers.

I was constantly amazed at the camaraderie, the energy, and the variety of personalities. Cocky? There's probably never been a cockier team. The Orioles didn't walk, they swaggered. They'd just blown out the Reds in the 1970 World Series, and would make it to the Series again come October 1971.

Cursing? I thought I'd heard it all, but this was the major league of profanity. Whenever someone delivered an especially lethal zinger, the place would erupt in laughter. I can still hear it: Paul Blair had a high-pitched cackle, almost like an air-raid siren. Cuellar's laugh sounded like an Amazon bird—"Aiy-yi-yi-yi!"

Earl Weaver was the cockiest of all. He was not a beloved figure. He had a blistering mouth, which was hilarious if it wasn't aimed at you. He was sarcastic and snide, and constantly berated players and umpires. Earl hated to lose even spring training games, and he was thrown out more than once.

Paul Blair was the coolest. He was very sharp with the ladies, and had a never-ending rap. He was an expert on everything.

Jim Palmer was very self-assured and graceful. He kept his feelings inside, always in control. I never saw him perturbed.

Boog was the country boy, Li'l Abner. He kept the clubhouse stereo cranking with country music all day long.

Mark Belanger and Davey Johnson, the double-play combo, were like twins, always together. They were the thinkers, constantly talking shop.

Frank Robinson was just like he is now: no nonsense. Not a jerk, but very standoffish. His body language spoke loudly: "I am Frank Robinson. Do not engage me in casual conversation."

There was a strict caste system. Rookies like Don Baylor and Bobby Grich were treated like dirt, but veterans had the status of kings. Frank was the most illustrious vet, a great player and a strong personality near the end of his career. He never rode the team bus to away games, always drove his own car. And Earl never, ever messed with Frank.

Brooks Robinson? Absolutely, positively the most decent of them all, and maybe of all the athletes I've met since. Ballplayers have to autograph dozens of baseballs in the clubhouse every day. Most players delegate that responsibility to the batboys. I signed various Orioles' names on hundreds of balls. Brooks *always* signed his own.

Brooks would always invite me to play catch or pepper with him and the other players, and to sit with him on bus rides. He was exactly what I pictured a sports hero to be, yet he was simply a good friend.

Gordon Beard once wrote, "They name candy bars after Reggie

Jackson, they name kids after Brooks Robinson."

Years later I would name my son after Brooks. Since my wife is Japanese and her relatives can't pronounce Brooks, we made it my son's middle name.

When the Orioles broke camp and headed north that spring, and again the following spring, I cried.

I've been on stage with Frank Sinatra, I've performed with Loretta Lynn at the Grand Ole Opry. But those two springs I had with the Orioles were the most exciting times of my life.

After two months as an Oriole, it was very dull going back to the real world. I had to find a way to stay in sports and meet more of these people. I knew I wasn't ever going to be a ballplayer, but there had to be other ways.

I went on to college at the University of Miami, and by the age of twenty-one, I was the sports anchor at TV station WPLG. I walked into that same Orioles' clubhouse six springs later, a professional broadcaster. A lot of the same guys were there, Brooks and Boog and Palmer, but it was different.

Now I was the media. I realized that I would never again be one of the guys.

That was okay, because I was no longer the starry-eyed fan. And even though I would never again be part of a team like I was those two springs in Miami, the cigars, pine tar, and Bazooka still smelled sweet.

And still do.

And the sports and the people still hold a fascination for me. I've interviewed what seems like a million of them, I hope to interview a million more, and I'd like to share with you some of my most memorable moments.

OZONE ALL-STARS

There is a special place in my heart for the athletes who live on the outskirts of reality. This is a select band of eccentrics whose elevators not only go to the top floor, but keep right on going.

I love these guys, all of them, for their steadfast refusal to be like everyone else, and to be the way they are without trying, because most of them don't consider themselves odd.

Wilt Chamberlain, for instance, sees himself as a normal fellow adrift in a world of abnormal people. By the way, it is with sincere apologies, but with profound respect, that I include Mr. Chamberlain in this discussion.

Superstars tend to lead normal superstar lives when they retire. They make the rounds of the autograph shows and oldtimers' games, they get into businesses built around their names and generally live out their days as ceremonial retired gods.

Wilt is in his very own post-fame groove. He is not ceremonial. He's not even retired, although some might say he has retired himself to stud.

He turned fifty-six in August 1992, he plays competitive beach volleyball and tennis, rides a mountain bike, and still believes he could play NBA basketball. I do not dispute that belief.

Wilt remains a bachelor, as he reminded us in 1992, casually mentioning that he has gone to bed with at least twenty thousand women, though not all of them at the same time.

In a way, I feel sorry for Wilt. Most American sports heroes are admired and loved, but I don't think Wilt ever achieved the "loved" part, unless you count those twenty thousand close personal friends.

A lot of it has to do with his size. As he says, nobody loves Goliath. Think about it. Name one physically huge superstar, in any sport, who was truly loved. Kareem? Great respect, but never really loved.

Wilt is a shade over seven feet tall, which isn't really that big anymore. But he was always considered a giant. Even today, his name is synonomous with bigness.

Wilt is a presence. He's not a menacing guy at all, but he scares people. Maybe it's his utter self-assurance and ease. Unlike most tall guys, you'll never see Wilt hunched over, trying to look smaller. He has a grace that is very unusual for a man his size. Also, he is the one huge man I've met whose voice is as big as he is. Wilt isn't afraid to make himself heard.

On the court he played more like an eight-footer with a six-footer's dexterity. Most huge players tend to be stand-around blocks of granite. Wilt was one of the fastest players in the NBA in his day, faster than most of the point guards, and one of the great leapers of any time, any size. There are only two or three men in history who could pluck a coin from the top of the backboard, thirteen feet in the air. Wilt could do it with ease.

And strength? One reporter recalls seeing Wilt hold a bowling ball in each hand, his arms spread to the sides, palms down and without using the finger holes. Wilt never fought on the court and wasn't into physical intimidation, but because he was so big and strong, he was seen as the ultimate bully. Critics said he scored all those points and got all those rebounds just because he was bigger than everyone, which was rubbish.

But I don't need to defend Wilt. He does a great job of that himself.

I'm glad I'm alive to talk about him after what I did to him one day many years ago. I used to do my daily run on the Drake Stadium track at UCLA, and I would see Wilt all the time. He's a big track fan, so he'd be running or working with the young women on the track team he sponsors. He knew me because I was a sportscaster on CBS in Los Angeles, and we struck up a friendship.

I found him to be imposing, but only physically. He can put you at ease quickly, and he's fun to be around. He's always ready to discuss and debate whatever is going on in the world.

One night I was working the Sunkist Invitational indoor track meet at the Los Angeles Sports Arena. Naturally Wilt was there, and he agreed to do a live interview with me at 6:20.

The guys on my camera crew were thrilled.

"Wow, do you think we can get Wilt's autograph?"

Just before the interview I found Chamberlain and asked him, "Wilt, would you do me a favor?"

"Sure, my man. What do you have in mind?"

"When you come over for the interview, whatever I say, just play along, okay?"

"Uh, okay."

Wilt showed up at 6:15 for the 6:20 live shot. I shook my head.

"You know what Wilt?" I said. "I've had it with you. I'm sick and tired of this b.s. I told you to be here at 6:10, not 6:15."

"M-my man, I'm sorry . . ."

"Look! I don't want your apologies. You asked me if you could do this interview, so I'm doing it as a favor to you. But no more."

The two guys on the crew were ashen. We did the interview, Wilt was great. When we finished my cameraman and soundman were looking at me like I was crazy. I looked at them and shrugged, "Hey, guys like this you've got to keep in line." Then I couldn't help it, I busted up and so did Wilt.

Later I thanked him for doing the interview and for going along with the corny joke.

"Firestone, I almost killed you. I knew what you were doing, but I could've put you through that wall, you know."

I know.

Chamberlain has been on the show several times. Once he came on barefooted. Wilt marches to his own wardrobe drummer, too.

He thinks "formal attire" means a black tank-top. Because most guests come on the show wearing shoes, I felt Wilt's bare feet were worth mentioning. He picked up one foot and stuck it about an inch from the camera lens.

An ant's eye view of Wilt Chamberlain. Eat your heart out, PBS.

I asked Wilt about his unusual whims, why he'll sometimes take off and drive cross-country, nonstop, at breakneck speed.

"You're right when you say 'whim,' " he said. "I love a drive, see, but I love to be alone. I've always driven by myself, I've gone across country twenty times, maybe. Always alone."

What do you think about when you drive?

"Oh, a number of things. Who I am, what I'd like to be, I think about goin' fast, doing things that you shouldn't be doing, maybe a little faster than you should be going, flirting with, not with death, but just those things that seem to be what we like to do but we're afraid of. I water ski at over one hundred miles an hour. When I drive my cars, I've gone as much as 180 miles an hour. Most people dream of doing those things, but never have enough nerve, maybe, to try them."

That's what Wilt is: a test pilot for fun and games. The rest of us can get our kicks vicariously through him. Like the twenty thousand sexual conquests. Not that that all of us aspire to that kind of goal, but most of us have less fun in life than we'd like to. Wilt maxes out the fun meter.

I asked Wilt if twenty thousand was a conservative estimate, since he started his conquests at age fifteen.

"I would say it's conservative, and I would also have to say [age] fifteen may be high. I might've started a little earlier. I've been around."

He took exception to my use of the term "conquest."

"Let me say one thing. It was never a conquest. It was a mutual consent, where our minds both wanted something and our bodies did it, understand? I never looked upon it as a conquest, it was the enjoyment of a sexual encounter. Many of these ladies are my friends today."

How many of them would you remember?

"I could remember maybe fifteen thousand. And all the names I would see, I would remember."

No one-night stands?
"I didn't say that. Maybe even some one-hour stands."

What do you think it's like to be with Wilt for a night?
"Let me just clear one thing up. For me not to have mentioned a number in my book would've been ludicrous. To be involved with twenty thousand or so ladies consumed as much of my time as my whole basketball career. If I'd have left my basketball career out of this book, I might as well have left this number out. I used the number only to explain to people just how involved I was.

"If I told you I scored a lot of points in basketball, it may be fifteen points a game, or ten. Give some numbers, so people understand what you're talking about. I'm not talking about it in a braggadocious manner, I'm talking about it as a fact, so that people can understand what 'a lot' is, or how much it consumed of your life."

I asked him about the type of women he preferred.

"I have been very fortunate, I think, on the physical scale. Most people would see me with a date, they would say, hey, she's a nine or a ten. So yes, I've been very very lucky."

We talked once about his never having had a serious relationship of any duration. Would he ever marry?

"I never believe in closing the door, I never say never. I'm from a very successful family, as far as marriage is concerned. My mother and father have been married for almost fifty years, and I have a great deal of respect for the institution, but I think in today's world, there's almost no place for it."

I believe that when Wilt is eighty years old, or one hundred, he'll still be chasing women—and catching them—and he'll still be taking shots at his two old basketball rivals, Bill Russell and Kareem Abdul-Jabbar. You can always get a rise out of Chamberlain just by mentioning either of those names.

In truth, the rivalries were sparked by the other guys. Wilt befriended Kareem when he was in high school, yet Kareem turned on Wilt, criticizing him viciously in his book as a whiner and a quitter. Russell, too, took shots at Wilt years ago, calling him a quitter.

"Athletes have a lot of pride," Chamberlain said. "We are very competitive, and Kareem and I are natural rivals. I would love to be more friendly with Kareem.

"Russell and I were very very close at one time, and Russell had some statements to make when he got out of basketball that were very unkind to me. He apologized through the press a few years later, but never to me."

One thing that probably got Kareem's hackles up was Wilt's public support of Richard Nixon for the presidency in 1968. I asked Wilt about Nixon.

"I would definitely support Nixon again, definitely, because I believed very very strongly at the time that Nixon was the best man for our country, the best at foreign affairs."

Wilt, of course, is the best at domestic affairs.

I've interviewed Nixon a couple times on the subject of baseball, and I'll tell you two things:

One, he knows the game.

Two, talking baseball to Richard Milhous Nixon was as close as I've come in TV work to an out-of-body experience. I felt like I was standing back watching myself talk baseball to a man impersonating Dick Nixon. Not only do you not expect a former leader of the Free World to be seriously discussing the merits of Mookie Wilson, but Nixon's mannerisms are so distinctive that he seems to be *doing* Nixon.

Nixon and I, you must understand, go back a long ways.

Nixon was my first impression at age ten or so. He was the easiest to do, and is still one of my favorites.

We finally met at the Republican National Convention in Miami Beach in 1972, although "met" probably isn't the right word. I was a teenage radical "wannabe," and he was the President of the United States, going for his second term. A couple of friends and I were among the protesters in the streets. One day Nixon's limousine cruised past and I tossed a rock at it.

Now we skip ahead to 1979, in the clubhouse of the California Angels on the night they won the Western Division title, beating the Royals.

I'm standing with Richard Crystal, Billy's brother, taking in the crazy scene, the champagne-squirting bedlam, and looking for people to interview on camera. Nixon is there, too, standing among the observers. He is a friend of Angels' owner Gene Autry. I ask Nixon if we can interview him. He says sure, and we roll the camera.

"Let me first say that I have always been an Angels fan," Nixon says, not wanting to appear a bandwagon-jumper.

Just then Angel infielders Jim Anderson and Rance Mulliniks, spot Nixon. As you know, nobody has diplomatic immunity in a winners' clubhouse. Anderson and Mulliniks run over and start gleefully pouring champagne on Nixon's head. He looks like he is standing under a foamy waterfall. Then, in baseball fashion, they start to tousle his hair, working in the champagne.

The stuff is stinging Nixon's eyes and he's lurching around like a blind man who has just been attacked. There are about six Secret Service agents on hand to protect Nixon, ultraserious fellows in short haircuts and suits, and they have no idea how to handle the situation. It is not in the official Secret Service handbook. Should they pounce on Anderson and Mulliniks and wrestle them to the ground? They're making frantic calls on their walkie-talkies.

Nixon is stunned, too. I'm pretty sure it's a new experience for him. But he realizes this makes him one of the guys, that it is a gesture of acceptance and affection and even respect. He just hunches his shoulders and says—you'll have to imagine the Nixon voice here—"Ahhh, champagne shampoo!"

The next time Nixon and I meet is during the 1986 World Series. My camera crew is set up in the lobby of the Waldorf-Astoria. I see Nixon and say, "Mr. President, would you like to talk a little about the World Series?"

Boom, we're off and running, two old chums talking ball. I hear myself telling him, "Sure, you say that about McDowell, but get him into a situation where he's gotta face Clemens . . ."

And he shoots back, "Well, you know, Roy, I've watched this platooning situation between Mookie and Dykstra, and I've felt this way: If the Sox go with the righthander, you wanna jam those Mets outfielders, try to pitch them inside and tight, but you don't have anybody on the Red Sox who can do that, maybe Bruce

Hurst . . . You know, on the natural turf, it's a different story, as opposed to when you play somewhere like Busch Stadium, and you don't want to get into a situation where Hernandez is on base, he can't run like he used to . . ."

I realized that for Nixon, baseball is no different than military strategy. Analyzing the Mets is like figuring out how to mine Haiphong Harbor.

I also realize that we're like two guys in a bar, and an old cliché suddenly rings true about baseball being America's common denominator, a common language and body of knowledge. It's some kind of spiritual thing, I guess, but it's hard to have bad feelings about someone with whom you're talking ball. There was no greater Nixon foe at my high school or college than me, I detested everything he stood for, but now I can hang with him.

"What was your team, growing up?" Nixon asks me.

I tell him the Orioles and Nixon says, "Ah, they had a good staff, they had Cuellar, Dave McNally, they had Palmer, and who was the other one?"

I remind him it was Pat Dobson.

"Ahhh, the Dobber."

The Dobber!

"They had four twenty-game winners one year, didn't they? Just goes to show you. Even with all they had, they still got beat in seven by the Pirates."

I suddenly feel myself hovering above the scene, watching myself and Nixon, schmoozing, arguing, matching baseball knowledge and insight. I'm thinking, "It's really him, this is not a cartoon or an impression."

He goes on: "You talk about an Oil Can Boyd . . . ," and the idea of Nixon even saying "Oil Can Boyd" strikes me as hilarious.

And he knows his stuff. He isn't just spitting out factoids and memorized stats, but making interesting applications of his knowledge, speculating, opinionizing.

This guy would have made a great baseball manager. He has the basic knowledge, and obviously feels comfortable being in charge. He has all the tools: the ability to schmooze with the press, yet to sometimes be suspicious and paranoid. He has a gift for diplomacy and the guts to try the occasional unusual maneuver, to go against the book. He'd be stealing signs, pulling hit-and-runs, sending in surprise relief pitchers. Tricky Dick, they'd call him.

Nixon might have have been happier in that line of work. He loves being around the game. He seems like a guy who, as a kid, was the last one picked for the team. He had all the answers in school and he wasn't popular. But now, as an adult, he is allowed inside the baseball world, and is respected for his opinions.

Keith Hernandez told me he had lunch at Rusty Staub's restaurant in New York with Staub and Nixon. Keith said he'd ask Nixon political questions and Nixon would ask him baseball questions.

It was a treat for Hernandez and Staub, but I'll bet anything that Nixon was enjoying it even more, being one of the boys.

I interviewed Nixon again when his library was dedicated in the summer of 1992. We did an hour, two shows' worth, and I have to admit I thoroughly enjoyed it. If you'd told me twenty years earlier that I would be sitting with Dick Nixon in his presidential library, posing for pictures and getting his autograph, I would have been astounded.

But there we were. On the air he named his all time all star teams, from three different eras, and we debated some of the picks. He had Mike Schmidt at third base on the modern-era team, and I lobbied for Brooks Robinson. He had Mays in center field, and I favored Aaron.

I forgot all about Watergate and the enemies list and the eighteen-minute gap on the tape and all my friends who were sent to Vietnam, although none of that stuff is trivial, certainly. It's just that I saw another side of this person I once saw as pure evil.

I asked him a question about forgiveness, because if anybody embodies the need and desire to be forgiven, it's Nixon. He said George Steinbrenner, Mike Tyson, and Pete Rose should all be forgiven, and that Rose should be in the Hall of Fame. Nixon and Rose are similar: neither ever said "I'm sorry," although Nixon at least showed some contrition.

"Well, I think the American people are a very fair people," he said. "They understand that sometimes those who will not meet the standards they feel are proper, once they have taken whatever punishment they have had to take, they welcome them back into the fold."

The only people to whom Nixon didn't seem willing to extend the olive branch of forgiveness were druggies, like Steve Howe, and steroid abusers. I guess there are dirty tricks and then there are dirty tricks.

Anyway, I think we had some kind of rapport going, we got pretty chummy, and as I was leaving he told me, "You know, I really enjoy the show you do with your dad every year."

He happened to notice I had four baseballs in my hand and said, "Would you like me to sign those?"

The show aired a week later, and the next day I got a phone call from one of Nixon's aides. He said Nixon loved the show and wanted to get a tape of it, and wanted permission to put the tape on a video loop and play it continuously at the library, for visitors. I think he wants the American people to see that he's just a regular guy.

Regular guy? Nixon? My God, what am I saying?

I guess it's a good thing there's no Vegas-style marquee in front of the Nixon Library. I can see it now: NIXON AND FIRESTONE TALK BALL!

Fred Dryer is a kid's toy that you wind up and let go. He takes off in some crazy directions and never stops. Fred retired from pro football in 1981, and more people think of him as Rick Hunter, the no-nonsense TV cop. But I never met a more amusing guy.

When Fred played for the Giants at the beginning of his NFL career, he actually lived in a Volkswagen van for a time. He was one of the league's best defensive ends, even though he played at an absurdly light 220 pounds. Fred pretty much follows his own itinerary.

I was interviewing him one afternoon at the Rams' camp in Anaheim. It was a hot day. Practice had just ended, and he stripped off his jersey as he walked over to do the interview.

My soundman handed Dryer a microphone, the kind that you attach to the front of your shirt with an alligator clip. Fred took the mike and clipped it to his left nipple, and we did the interview.

People tell me that he is pain in the ass to work with on *Hunter*, which he produced for three years. They say he fires directors and terrorizes the other actors. I have no reason to doubt that. But the Dryer I know is the guy who reminds me of the old saying, "I once was disgusted, but now I'm amused."

All during his football career, I'm sure he saw plenty to be disgusted about, saw a lot of friends get shredded and spit out by the NFL meatgrinder. But I always had the sense that he was in it for the ride, for the adventure. Indiana Jones in cleats and pads.

I know this: Fred is his own man, and he does not kiss butt. A lot of guys say that about themselves, which usually means it's not true. Fred never says that about himself.

In one interview with him, I was trying to do my Sigmund Freud thing.

"You know what, Fred," I said, "I think you're awfully confused about life."

He looked at me and shot back, "I'm not confused at all. I know exactly what I want from life, and how to get it."

A lot of people would say that because it sounds good, but with him it rang true. He probably hasn't reevaluated his life ten times. It's all very clear to him. He knows what he wants and he knows how to get it.

I guess it was me who was confused about him being confused.

On our show, Fred is a broken-field runner. Give him the ball and he will find the holes, talk to daylight. One day I asked him about sportswriters. You should know that many athletes barely are aware that sportswriters are real people, and fewer still have any concept of what it is sportswriters actually do. Fred had obviously studied the breed, and though I don't necessarily agree with his blanket evaluation, it was stunning in its detail.

"I think sportswriters are a lot of laughs," he said, "and here's why. Doug Krikorian (then an L.A. sportswriter) called me up on a Monday after a game in Atlanta. We'd won, barely, but we'd won, so he calls me up Monday at my house, says, 'Now that everyone else is finished talking to you, tell me what really happened in the game.'

"I started laughing and said, 'Doug, this is preposterous. Here's how I look at you guys. You get a free ride come Friday to whatever city we're playing in. You get fed, get to hang around with your heroes, you get to go out and get bleepin' drunk Friday night.

" 'Saturday you're free, you have brunch, right? You get to stuff your face, you get to go to practice, you get to see us laugh, you're in on all the jokes, you know who the putz of the team is, you know a lot of top secrets, we trust you with that, and then they put you on a bus and take you back to the hotel.

" 'Saturday night you go out and get slammed again, you go to bed at four in the morning, get up at eight, go out and catch another free brunch, you hit the stadium, you load up on dogs and beer, get your 50-yard-line seat, you got your typewriter, your computer, your go-fer, your pencils and your ink and for three hours you're sitting there, telling us about the game.

" 'Then the game is over with, you hit the press elevator, you go down to the locker room, you walk in and you say, "What happened?" Then a good guy like me says, "Here's what happened," and you write it down and say, "I don't believe you." And then you have the guts to call me and wake me up Monday morning. Get outta here.' "

Another time Fred told a story about his encounters with another Ozone All-Star, Andy Warhol.

"I remember one time going to his studio in New York City, having lunch with him, seeing all his stuff, talking with him for a couple of hours, going outside in the street and taking strange photographs of cars and buildings and stuff. Warhol wasn't like anything I've ever seen. He was a very sensitive guy, and not a sports fan.

"Then in 1980 I was with the Rams and we went back to New York to play the Giants. I was with (Rams defensive end) Mike Fanning, an Okie from Tulsa, and I said, 'Look, I have to go into the City 'cause Andy's going to interview me at a restaurant.' He said, 'Can I go with you?' and I said sure. After practice we took a cab from the Meadowlands into the city.

"Mike said, 'Gee, Andy Warhol—is that the guy with the funny hair?' And I said yeah. We got to the restaurant, sat down at the table, and there were a bunch of people from *Interview* magazine. He put me on the cover. Andy didn't say anything during the interview. It's an on-going conversation, and he just presses the button on his tape recorder and whatever is said is printed. It's not edited.

"It's all really fun. We start talking, and now Mike is looking around at these strange guys. There's two guys with Andy, he's sitting in the corner, they're just sitting there with their arms folded, and every once in a while they'd look at one another and point to Mike. Now Mike is eating caviar off this little tiny plate, he's eating salad and he notices them looking at him and he looks at me.

"And then Andy takes a little pixie camera from under the table and takes a picture of Mike. These two other guys are gay as the wind and the *other* two guys, who the hell knew who they were? They were probably driving the limousine. The whole interview took place, and Mike ate seventy-five stacks of salads, 'cause they were on these really small plates, and everyone was looking at him, 'cause he was way bigger than me and they thought *I* was big.

"Then we went outside and I said, 'Goodbye, Andy, see you later,' and he said, 'Thanks a million guys, you were so fabulous.' I offered him two tickets to the game and he said, 'Gee, I've never been to a sporting event in my life. I don't want to sit up there with those people.' So they said goodbye and got into the limo and drove off.

"I said, 'Let's go, Mike,' and he says, 'I just want to tell you something, Fred. Andy Warhol shows up in Tulsa, he gets his ass kicked.' "

At the end of the show I was signing off and I thanked Dryer for being on the show. He looked at me very seriously and said, "Thank you, Roy. Stay out of Tulsa."

THREE

A WAY
WITH WORDS

Bleeps, bloops and blunders? We've had a few, some unusual and unexpected moments that jump out of my mental scrapbook.

Like the time Dexter Manley, the great but troubled former lineman of the Redskins, was on the show to promote his autobiography, *Educating Dexter,* which he co-wrote with sportswriter Tom Friend.

It's an interesting book in which Dexter deals candidly with his many demons—childhood poverty, drugs, illiteracy, and wives who surprise you in bed with twins.

Normally I don't pry deeply into the sex lives of my guests, but Dexter was fair game, since the incident with the twins was in the book and he was on the show promoting that same book.

"Dexter," I said, "I want to ask you about the chapter that deals with your stormy first marriage. You talk about some of your extracurricular sexual escapades, and there's mention of your wife catching you in bed with twins."

Dexter's eyes got as big as hubcaps. It's the kind of reaction I would expect if I put the same question to President Clinton.

Manley looked around nervously and said, "What? What are you talking about?"

I could see the fear in his eyes, so I asked, "Isn't that right?"

"No!" he said. "It is absolutely wrong. I don't know where you got that, but your facts are wrong, completely erroneous and misleading, and I would like to stop taping right now!"

We never stop tape, but obviously something was very wrong, so I signaled for the cameras to shut down.

Tom Friend had come to the studio with Dexter and was watching the taping from behind camera. He jumped up and said, "Dex, don't you remember? Chapter Ten? Where we talk about that stuff?"

"Yeah!" Dexter said, indignantly, "but they weren't twins. There was three girls."

"Then what you're saying, Dex," I said, "is that I was only numerically incorrect?"

"Yeah!" he said.

I asked him, "Don't you feel that this kind of thing is a bit titillating?"

Dexter shot back, "What's that mean?"

"Not what you *think* it means," I said. "In this case it means you have a sexual escapade that you sensationalize just to sell a book."

"Well," Dexter said, "they *was* sensational."

So we went back to taping and I corrected my error on camera. *Three* girls. I didn't bother to ask Dexter if they were triplets.

Before I met Dexter, years ago, I had been warned about his language. This was just before my first live interview with Dexter, in 1987. I was doing NFL football commentary for ESPN's *Game Day* show in Ft. Lauderdale, and Dexter was my live in-studio guest.

Manley, I want to stress, is a delightful guest, a genuinely warm and funny and likable man. But he is not always careful of his language.

"Roy," the producer told me, "don't let this guy use any swear words live on the air."

"No problem," I told him confidently. "I'll talk to Dex."

Soon Manley arrived.

Dexter: "Oh man, I'm so glad to be here, I'm so glad to be doin' the show."

Me: "Dex, I really appreciate you coming on. There's one thing I do want to run by you. I know you would never do anything like this, but we'll be on live, so you can't use any bad words."

Dexter: "Oh. Okay. Like what words?"

Me: "Well, obviously don't say —— or ——, things like that."

Dexter: "Oh, man, you think I would do that?"

Me: "Dex, it's a standard thing, we tell this to all the guests, just to remind them the show is going out live to the entire nation."

Dexter: "Gotcha."

We got on the air. I jumped into my first question.

Me: "Dexter, you've had a little battle with the writers in D.C. Could you talk a little about your relationship with the sportswriters?"

Dexter: "Well, you know, most writers is assholes."

(My producer was screaming into my earpiece. "Cut him off! Stop him!")

Me: "Uh, Dex, I think you might want to put that another way."

Dexter: "Oh, I'm sorry, Roy. I wasn't supposed to say asshole, was I? I meant to say pricks. They're mostly pricks."

I am positive Dexter was not trying to be a wise guy, or sabotage the show.

"Well," he continued, "a lot of the pricks that come to interview me . . ."

The director was screaming in my ear for me to cut off every answer, but every time I cut one off, Dexter would go on to the next thought, using even saltier language.

It was a lively interview.

We don't get many medical breakthroughs on the show, but I think we've been close a couple times.

Once I had a major league baseball coach as a guest and he was praising the courage of one of his team's pitchers. This pitcher was so ill that he had to be given fluids intravenously, yet he went out an hour later and pitched a shutout.

"This guy is so tough," the coach said, "that he pitched right after having an IUD put in him."

I was at a loss for words. You might say there was a pregnant pause.

On another show, Red Schoendienst, then manager of the Cardinals, was talking about a similar situation with a different pitcher.

"This guy was so dehydrated," Red said, "that he had an RV stuck in his arm."

Red must have been referring to the condition known as Winnebago Elbow.

Seeking an existential look into the psyche of Pete Rose, I asked him, "How would you have been as a woman?"

Said Rose: "I'd have been an ugly one."

And going deep with George "The Thrill" Will, political columnist and author of *Men At Work*, I asked George to give me his take on how certain political figures might fare in baseball.

George Bush.

"George Bush, remember, threw left and batted right. You don't want to do that, it's just wrong. He's a good utility infielder, and that's what he should have been."

Ted Kennedy as a manager.

"Well, I don't think he'd enforce a rigorous curfew."

Boris Yeltsin as a manager.

"I think he managed the Orioles once, under the name Earl Weaver. Same sort of ebullient, populist approach to the world."

Margaret Thatcher as manager.

"Well, she has kind of the icy demeanor of a Gene Mauch, and the iron will of a John McGraw."

Fidel Castro. How might he manage?

"Briefly, I hope. Here's a man who speaks in four-hour paragraphs. He could never deliver the lineup card."

Sam Donaldson, what kind of baseball man?

"He played second base for the Giants. Eddie Stanky. Feisty, scrappy, a nondenominational nihilist. Mean to everybody, regardless of race, color or creed."

Old joke: Man and woman in bed. They hear the woman's husband at the front door.

Man: "Quick, where's your back door?"

Woman: "We don't have one."

Man: "Where would you like one?"

Which brings us to Kirk Gibson, the fastest guest in the history of the show.

Kirk and I were getting the countdown to start the show when a huge earthquake struck the Southland. The studio rumbled and shook, the ground quivered and a huge rack of lights over our heads began to tremble.

Being a longtime California guy, I knew what to do—sit frozen in fear, waiting for a thousand pounds of lights to fall on my head.

Gibson, being a Michigan boy, wasn't hip to earthquake procedure. He bolted out of the chair like he was getting a jump on a sinking line drive.

He had a microphone clipped to his shirt, the cord running inside the shirt. The mike went with him, along with an entire deck of audio cables which were torn out of the control panel.

Gibson nearly ran through a brick wall on his way out of the building. I pictured him putting a cartoon-like hole in the wall, and future guests saying, "Funny, but that door reminds me of Kirk Gibson."

Jose Canseco is a tough guy to book on the show, but we finally got him, in the winter of 1991. For some reason he was staying in Thousand Oaks, forty miles from the studio.

Just as our driver picked Canseco up, the sky fell. The worst rainstorm in about three decades hit the city. Roads were flooded. Along the coast highway, a motorhome was washed out to sea.

I wouldn't have blamed Jose if he'd told the driver to turn around and take him back, but he pressed on. Jose and the driver were stuck on the freeways for four and a half hours.

A lot of guests come on the show to promote their latest gig, which is fine, but sometimes the promotion can backfire. Like the time our guest was Debi Thomas, the 1986 world champion figureskater.

Debi came on the show right after the 1988 Winter Olympics, where she had finished third. Thomas had just turned pro and was touring the country with the "Benson & Hedges on Ice" show.

I'm not a fiery-eyed antismoking crusader, but it occurred to me that this was an unusual situation—A fantastically conditioned and cleancut champion, who was also a premed student at Stanford, essentially selling cigarettes.

After all, according to the U.S. Center for Disease Control, more than fifty thousand women are dying of lung cancer each year. It has become the leading cancer killer of women, ahead of breast cancer. Women are the prime target of cigarette companies because the advertisers play on the fears of getting fat, and on desire for independence.

I wondered if skating for a cigarette company presented a moral dilemma for Debi, so I read her some stats, that smoking causes more deaths than heroin, alcohol, and hundreds of other drugs combined. I also noted that Benson & Hedges had pledged $100,000 from tour profits to the homeless. Then I asked her:

Nevertheless, the question of the athlete, of the entertainer, is the responsibility to the impressionable audience, and that is the one we're going to raise right now. At what point did you say, "Hmmm, I'm an athlete, I'm a role model, and a premed student. I know cigarettes are bad for people. Can I reconcile this for myself?"

Debi replied, "Well, I think the thing you have to emphasize is that the skaters are not promoting cigarettes in any way. We just happen to have Benson & Hedges as a sponsor.

"I know plenty of doctors who still smoke. The whole idea of it is that it is for a good cause as far as benefiting the homeless, and once we go out there to skate, I think people are more concentrating on our skating than on cigarettes or smoking. We're not there to promote the cigarettes."

I guess the bigger question is, is it too much to expect or ask of athletes to represent all things to all people?

"People that smoke are going to smoke, and people that don't smoke are not going to smoke. I don't think in any way, for people that already smoke, that are already going to kill themselves, maybe they'll switch to Benson & Hedges just because of the show, but I don't think anybody that doesn't smoke is going to switch."

Debi mentioned that it was hard for Scott Hamilton to agree to do the tour because his mother died of cancer from smoking.

We were taping the show, remember. When we went to a commercial, the PR person from Benson & Hedges, who was escorting Debi on her round of interviews, shot out of her chair like she'd sat on a lighted Benson & Hedges.

The PR person's function in such situations is to make sure the sponsor is not only recognized during the interview, but presented in a favorable light. Mentioning the product in terms of lung cancer probably isn't considered favorable.

I can still see the frozen smile on the PR lady's face. Fear? Paranoia? Anger? All of the above?

"Debi," the woman said, "I'm sure you didn't mean to say what you said. I'm sure what you meant to say is that smoking is a freedom of choice decision that you don't want to judge. Right, Debi?"

This ticked Debi off.

"I said exactly what I meant," she said. "What do you think, that I smoke?"

"But Debi," the woman said, "you know our show is sponsored by Benson & Hedges, right?"

"I know that," Debi said. "You think I don't know that? You

think that I smoke cigarettes? I don't smoke."

The woman turned to me, smile still locked in place, and said, "Of course we'll edit that out."

"Of course we *won't,*" I said.

"Well then, the interview is over," she said.

"No," I said, "the interview is still on."

I felt the point had been made, and I didn't want to get Debi fired from her first professional gig, so when we were back on camera, I said,

One thing I want to clarify in this conversation you made a statement that anyone that smokes and wants to kill themselves might switch to Benson & Hedges. Let's try to clarify that a little. It perhaps may have been abrupt.

"Yes, well, I didn't mean that, but everyone knows that smoking is an addiction, it's a habit . . . Some people chew gum, some people eat. And so it's just a choice. People have the choice to do whatever they want to do."

I don't know if that mollified the PR lady, but I'm guessing that Debi and I made few friends in the cigarette industry.

We don't usually have hecklers in our studio audience, because we don't have a studio audience. However, on one occasion the guest brought his own heckler.

Isiah Thomas was telling me about a controversial speech he had given at his old college, Indiana. During the speech he had mentioned that he learned a lot from coach Bobby Knight. Before the large, mixed audience, Isiah impersonated Knight using very bad language.

Isiah was basically defending himself to me, rationalizing his behavior at the speech, when we heard shouting. It was Isiah's mother, Mary, who was sitting behind the cameras.

"You messed up!" she yelled. "You were bad. You shouldn't have done that! That was wrong!"

And so on. Her words were easily picked up by our microphones, so Isiah, on the air, shrugged and smiled and said, "My mom's here, and she's right. I messed up."

I have learned to be very careful with names. Verrrry careful. Mixups can happen. For example:

In 1976, I was a TV sports anchor in Miami. I had recently graduated from the University of Miami, where I had become good friends with Rubin Carter, the Hurricanes' great defensive lineman.

Rubin was playing in the NFL by then, but he was back in Miami and he phoned my place, wanting to get together for a beer.

I happened to be sharing an apartment with a guy who was not a sports fan. I was at work so he answered the phone.

Coincidentally, in the papers that very same morning was a big news story about Rubin "Hurricane" Carter, the former boxer, who had been paroled that morning from prison. "Hurricane Carter," you may remember, was sent up the river for a shotgun murder, but with the help of celebrities such as Bob Dylan, Carter got retried and finally released. That very day.

Anyway, my old college pal Rubin phoned. He has a very deep, intimidating voice. When my roommate told him I was at work, Rubin said, "Just tell Roy that Rubin Carter called and that I'm lookin' for him."

My roommate, remembering the news story, asked, "Is this Rubin "Hurricane" Carter?"

And Carter, faithful alum, said, "Yeah, this is Rubin Carter, the Hurricane."

Now my roommate figured it was actually me on the phone, doing an impression of the paroled ex-boxer.

"Right, Rubin," my roommate said. "Murder anyone lately?"

Carter was puzzled, and a little angry. My roommate realized it *wasn't* me. He panicked, hung up the phone, called the cops, then called me at work and said, "You won't believe who called. Did you badmouth "Hurricane" Carter on your TV show or something?"

I said, "No, why?"

He said, "Because he's looking for you, and he's pissed off."

Well, we sorted it out and called off the cops and everything was okay. You'd think a weird coincidence like this would only happen to you once.

Now we fast-forward to 1984, and Julius Erving is to be my guest on *SportsLook.* He's going to come on with his attorney, Irwin Weiner, so we can talk about sports business, and meet the man behind Dr. J.

We always send a limo to pick up our guest, because we have found that this greatly increases the chances of the guest actually showing up.

This particular day, for some reason, Dr. J and his attorney were staying at different Hyatt hotels, of which there are several in the greater Los Angeles area.

One limo driver picked up Doc at his Hyatt near the airport, and he arrived at the studio in plenty of time.

The driver who was to pick up Irwin Weiner somehow went to the wrong Hyatt Hotel. The driver went into the lobby and held up a sign that read, "Mr. Weiner."

That hotel happened to be hosting a group of people in town for some kind of fabric convention. One of the guests was a man named Saul Weiner, who was supposed to be picked up in the lobby and driven to the fabric show, where he had some official function.

Saul Weiner saw our driver and said, "I'm Mr. Weiner."

Our driver asked, "Are you the Mr. Weiner who's in town to do the show?"

"Yes I am."

They got into the limo, and the conversation went something like this:

Driver: "So, tell me about Dr. J."
Saul: "Dr. J? Oh, I'm a big basketball fan, I like Dr. J a lot."
Driver: "I bet. What kind of guy is he?"
Saul: "I don't know. I'm sure he's a terrific guy."

The driver figured Mr. Weiner was being standoffish because he didn't want to discuss his client with a stranger, so the driver clammed up.

After a forty-minute ride they got to the studio. The driver led Saul Weiner to our set. I was talking to Erving when they walked in.

Saul saw Dr. J and was stunned.

"My God," he said. "We were just talking about Dr. J, and here he is!"

Now the driver was sure this guy was a sarcastic put-on artist.

I said, "Hi, I'm Roy Firestone. Who are you?"

Saul said, "I'm Mr. Weiner."

"Great," I said. "Doc will be on with me first, then after the first commercial, we'll bring you out."

Doc was just kind of staring.

Saul said, "Mr. Firestone, I know who you are, but where is the fabric show?"

Five minutes later Saul Weiner was back in the limo, autographed photo of Dr. J in hand, heading back to some Hyatt hotel.

We issued an all-points-bulletin for Irwin Weiner, but didn't find him. Maybe he got picked up by Saul Weiner's driver.

FOUR

ARTHUR ASHE

Someday, the sooner the better, a statue of Arthur Ashe will be placed at an appropriate site, such as at the U.S. Open stadium in Flushing Meadows.

Hey, dad, who's that skinny dude in marble?
That's Arthur Ashe, son.
He looks like a librarian. Was he a librarian?
He may have been that, too, for all I know. What he was, son, was a warrior.
Gedouttahere, Pop. Him? What wars did he fight?
We don't have that much time, son. It will be faster to tell you what wars he didn't *fight.''*

Arthur Ashe won thirty-three tennis tournaments in his career, including three Grand Slam titles. He beat Jimmy Connors to win the Wimbledon championship in 1975.

But when you sit down to list the accomplishments of Ashe's life, the tennis stuff probably doesn't make the Top Ten.

He helped destroy apartheid in South Africa by serving a major role in the artists-and-athletes boycott. In doing so, Ashe won the respect and praise of Nelson Mandela.

He fought racial discrimination in America, by speaking out and by writing brilliantly in the op-ed pages of major newspapers.

He was a leading figure in the battle against AIDS.

He was a historian, having written a three-volume history of the black athlete in America, *A Hard Road to Glory,* and having co-written a TV adaptation that won an Emmy.

He was a political activist. As recently as 1992, he was arrested in Washington D.C. for protesting the U.S. policy on Haitian refugees.

He was a thinker, a philosopher, a dreamer.

Arthur Ashe was everything you ever wanted in a sports champion, and more.

I have sports heroes, people I admire greatly for various reasons. Ashe is No. 1 on that ladder.

I mentioned a statue, and I hope we won't have to wait long for it. Arthur was one of those guys who won't be fully appreciated until we all sit down to pore over his box score. We will notice then that he kicked some major ass.

Arthur's problem, if it can be called a problem, was that he looked like a librarian, and he sounded like your high school Civics teacher.

His personality was so subdued and cool and measured and thoughtful that even when he was causing all kinds of trouble, he didn't seem like a troublemaker.

He sometimes came off as a dispassionate man, a scientist in a white lab coat observing the human race and the human condition.

Here's the kind of dispassionate man Arthur Ashe was: The most recent time Arthur was on the show, in November 1992, I asked him, since he was diagnosed in 1988 as having AIDS, if he had come to appreciate certain things more.

Ashe started laughing, and he spoke of his five-year-old daughter, Camera.

"I'll tell you what I really appreciate," he said, "and I thought about this the other night and I mentioned it to my wife. One of the biggest pleasures I can experience is seeing my daughter eat chocolate cake and ice cream.

"There is such a look of unmitigated, open-ended joy, the way she holds the spoon and eats, it makes my whole day."

That reminded me of an Ira Berkow column in the *New York Times,* in which Ashe's wife mentions that Arthur was looking at Camera one day and suddenly burst into tears. It was one of the very few times Jeanne had seen Arthur cry.

Many athletes would wince at having such a sensitive side of his personality exposed. Arthur smiled. "It just sort of happened," he said. "We were still living up in Mt. Kisco then, and I was just sitting there staring at her and just started crying."

What were you thinking?

"I was thinking what I think every day when I look at her, whether she's eating chocolate cake or not—that I might not see her graduate from high school, or receive her first Holy Communion, or get married, or see her children.

"You think about all those things. Certainly, most of the things I might miss are related to my daughter, no question about that."

Not that Ashe was wallowing in self-pity. He was not a "Why me?" kind of guy:

"I think it's really the wrong question to ask, because why *not* me? Which I think is what Magic Johnson is also trying to say now."

Rather than sinking into his illness, Ashe levitated above it. Played keepaway. He had told me that this AIDS clock that ticked inside him had heightened his energy, creativity, and resolve.

Ashe was on the show early in 1992, two months before the news of his AIDS leaked out. He knew he had it; we didn't. Looking back on that interview, it was like he was trying to tell us all something.

I said to him, "You're a man who savors your life fully. You love people and life, yet there seems to be a contradiction. Early in your life you visited cemetaries all the time, at age five you saw your grandfather in an open casket. Death has been a fascination of yours."

Ashe didn't blink. He said, "It has. One of my earliest recollections was my grandfather's funeral, and less than a year later my mother died. Later on, for a while, I just would not go to any funerals.

"I didn't go to my mother's funeral. I didn't go to my tennis mentor's funeral, R.W. Johnson; I didn't go to (UCLA Athletic Director) J.D. Morgan's funeral. I just couldn't go to funerals.

"Then I had my heart attack and started thinking about it again, and the notion or the feeling I'm left with now is that I'm always in a hurry, I want to get done what I want to get done, for fear that there might not be a tomorrow.

"My wife tries to work on me to understand that, hey, your prospects of living a long and healthy life are pretty good, because I do take care of myself, I do what my doctor tells me to do, and I should be around for a while."

If you could capsulize coming to grips with your own mortality, in a few moments—that's TV—can you characterize what it's like at thirty-six [the age at which Ashe had the first of his two heart attacks] to realize that we don't get out of here alive?

"Well, it was difficult to have the heart attack at such a relatively young age, but in a larger sense it forces you to have a much more realistic outlook on what's possible in the future, and it makes you address the question of, can you do what it takes now to give yourself the best chance of living the longest and healthiest of lives?

"And I think I was able to transform the discipline I had as an athlete in an individual sport to the rest of my life and to the business world, and that really has helped me quite a bit. I think, to a great degree, that's why I'm still here."

Some consider it a mark against Ashe that he was a nonthreatening presence. Unlike an Ali or a Jim Brown or a Spike Lee—three non-butt-kissers who rile people up—Ashe didn't provoke immediate anger or fear.

It was a matter of style. Ashe once told me that he was convinced that this internalizing of his frustration and anger and rage contributed to his heart problems.

"I prefer to think that it doesn't matter," he said, "that you do what you feel you have to do, and if bad health is one of the minor negative consequences, so be it."

Outwardly, Ashe had ultimate cool. He had it on the tennis court. His generation of tennis players was courtly, pardon the pun. In the early- and mid-Seventies, you could go a whole fortnight at Wimbledon without hearing a player scream lewd obscenities at a linesperson. Must have been weird.

Back then you tried to intimidate your opponent with composure, rather than with psychotic tantrums. Arthur was a gentleman.

Some blacks disrespected him because he seemed not angry enough, not black enough. Didn't even talk hip.

Many blacks who make it big in sports or business speak two languages—English, and the less proper street talk. In part, that bilingualism is a tool of survival, and of cultural identity.

That's fine. But Arthur, I believe, had only one language. I think he would have seen it as hypocritical, and demeaning to his audience, to speak one way to me and another way to the "boyz in the hood."

The irony is, Ashe was as tough as they come. He was as much about black success and pride and entrepreneurship as any activist.

He had the air of a man untouched by racial turmoil, but he had been there. Ashe once told me, "Every day I close my eyes and pray that people won't be as cruel to my children as they have been to me."

Though he'd had the two heart attacks and two heart-bypass operations—a double and a quadruple—and had AIDS, Ashe was anything but a frail armchair philosopher.

He headed up the Davis Cup boycotts of the Sixties, when people were getting killed for their beliefs. He protested the Vietnam war, even taking his reasoned arguments onto the campus of the Air Force Academy after being pointedly warned not to.

He railed at what he called "microwavable political statements." He talked about how the more difficult—but more effective—route was to work within the system, work for change, not necessarily quietly, but methodically, doggedly.

I had seen Ashe himself change over the years. When I first met him in Miami about 1975, I remember remarking to him what a great man I considered Ali to be.

Ashe looked at me and said, "Do you really think Ali is an important figure in the social order of things for black people?"

I said, "Absolutely," and he gave me the arched eyebrow.

"Roy," he said, "Muhammad Ali is a figure, a personality, he is a lot of things, but in terms of real progress and offering a real agenda for black people, he's nothing more than a lot of words. Real work is not being done by people like Muhammad Ali."

But a few years ago we discussed Ali again, and Ashe talked about how he had come to appreciate Ali, admire him for what he has done, for helping give the black man dignity and power, for standing tall and speaking out.

My most recent (and last) interview with Ashe was in November 1992, in New York City. I asked him if we could get together for an interview. It was the week of Magic Johnson's reretirement, and I wanted Ashe's thoughts on that event, and on life in general.

It was raining the day we were to tape, and Ashe phoned my hotel to say he couldn't make it. He didn't say why, but it occurred to me later that the rain might be a factor. To someone with a fragile immune system, rain can be a threat. Yet after some pleading on my part, Arthur relented and agreed to do the interview.

We sent a limo to pick him up. Then, a few minutes before we were to begin, I had the distinct displeasure of having to tell Arthur that, for reasons unknown, we had no camera crew.

I had the gall to ask him to come back the next day. Ashe's dance card was full, but he said sure, he would come back, and he did.

As always, he was completely candid and thoughtful. We talked about Mike Tyson's rape trial, and Ashe mentioned that, while he understood the reaction among many blacks who were saying Tyson was a black victim of white law, Ashe felt the real victim was the woman in question.

Black women are a minority within a minority.

"Yes. I completely agree with that. Some sociological studies now point to that.

"One set of numbers that has been very disturbing to me, since the mid-Eighties, is that one-third of all campus sexual assaults have been committed by athletes, and a large percentage of those have been committed by black athletes.

"And when you get right into it, what you find out is that a lot of these athletes, black and white, feel that they are immune from whatever penalties may accrue normally in a situation like that.

"They feel, 'Well, that's just mine for the taking, because I'm me and I'm excused.' It is part of a pattern that a lot of us would like to see reversed, but I don't think it's going to happen anytime soon, because that is a state of affairs in which all athletes in America are brought up."

Individual responsibility. Why can't we hammer home that rule, to take individual responsibility?

"That's the contention that Harry Edwards likes to make very loudly, in saying that none of us is really going to change until we get the individual to assume control and responsibility for what he or she does.

"But that's countenanced and sometimes refuted by those who say, 'Hey, now wait a minute, you're not taking into your argument the sociological background, of which Mike Tyson may be a perfect example—the wrong side of the tracks in Brooklyn. And that he never really got the street kid in him out of his system.'

"To that extent, unless someone remediates him along the way, and the remediation is continuous, he's going to be a recidivist, so to speak.

"So you never really come to closure, there are just those who don't want to lay that complete responsibility on the individual."

We talked about apartheid and South Africa, and Gary Player. I said to Ashe,

It was Gary Player's contention that he was perhaps a part of the system, but that he saw the error of his ways, he now knows that apartheid was wrong. But did he aid and abet the system, did he come to the realization too late?

"I think in some respects he did, yes. I have had some problems with Gary Player, which I am sure he has read about because I have made my views known.

"There was a time when, next to Christiaan Barnard, Gary

Player was the most well-known South African on the face of the earth. Period. And he enjoyed unbelievable adulation, a high visibility. And he could have done a lot of good with that visibility.

"I would like to have seen him a bit more out front, a bit more progressive about his views. To say, ex post facto, as apartheid is crumbling, that he knows it is wrong, it's tough for me to buy that."

What about when he says, "I'm just an athlete, I've done no one wrong, I've had black caddies, I've had black friends, I grew up loving the black culture." It's not enough?

"No, no. I've also heard, in my trips to South Africa and since, that many expatriates and white Africans say, 'I love my maid, I love my houseboy, I love the boy who tends to my garden.'

"They throw this word love around as if it were just an expendable commodity. But that's not what we're talking about. We're talking about respect, human parity. I never thought that most white South Africans, until recently, considered blacks on the same human par with the rest of them."

Nelson George of the Village Voice *said, "Magic Johnson did not become black until he announced he was HIV-positive, at least in the public eye." What do you think?*

"What he's saying is that you can buy your way out of the common rejection that most black people experience, if you make enough money. You can either cross over, like Diana Ross or Michael Jackson or Bill Cosby or Bryant Gumbel.

"Or you can, even at that socioeconomic level, proactively identify yourself with the black masses, but it just doesn't work that way when you have that much money. It's only when something like AIDS, identified with the black lower socioeconomic classes, happens to someone who had that much money and influence, then yes, there's this direct connection."

Who makes a difference, Arthur? I think you've been an activist, an advocate, I think you've stuck to your guns, I think you've maintained your dignity about sports and life. But who will carry the torch?

"I don't know . . . If you start off in an ordinary African-American social situation, and you wind up with more than two nickels to rub together, and you have a chance to be up there with a Babe Ruth or Joe DiMaggio, what is asked of you is that you be politically neutral. You neuter yourself, in a way. And it's very difficult to do that and not come under withering criticism (from blacks)."

Mort Sahl once said that it takes real courage to love some body—yourself, mankind. I think it also takes courage to respect— to respect women, for instance. Or the law, or yourself. What about the lack of respect that we all seem to be maintaining?

"You're talking on one hand about the wimp factor, in the sense that if you take respect a bit too far, some people believe, you may be viewed as a wimp. That has negative connotations.

"Then there's this new phrase, really an abbreviation, coined by the rap community—dissing. Which means disrespect. When you're on the short end of the stick, as African-Americans imagine themselves to be, and in most cases are, you get very very sensitive about the lack of respect. Extremely sensitive, even though it may come from your own kind.

"And that, I believe, is one of the reasons there is so much black-on-black crime. But it is a huge issue, emotionally, wrapped up in one's manhood, and that's why just two days ago, for almost no provocation, at Thomas Jefferson High School in New York, a kid just blew away two of his classmates—because he felt that they dissed him."

What have you come to know about mankind, about the races and the love and the lack of love between them?

"I think about that a lot, because except for track stars, possibly, we tennis stars have traveled to more different places in a very short period of time than any other athletes.

"People do have some commonalities, family beliefs, in spite of the fact that they may have been in a country that was Communist and repressed religion. But every place I went was provincial. Every place, there was somebody there, some group in that place, which, if transposed to America, would be the blacks of that group, or the Hispanics."

What does that say to you about the human condition?

"I don't know. It's just that everybody is looking for somebody to look down upon. That saddens me, but it also gives me a firsthand measuring stick when I come back to America and I feel that, well, somebody didn't do me right, or somebody dissed me, and I think it was for racial reasons, I've seen that happen to somebody in Japan, too, or Australia, or England, or France . . . I've seen it with my own eyes, so I look at it a little differently here."

Did Magic have a responsibility to stay on the AIDS commission, or was he right in quitting?

"What Magic did was juxtapose the idea of the publicity given to resignation from the AIDS Commission versus a real visibility that he could have given to the commission by staying on.

"The only added element I wish Magic would have attended to was in addition to saying 'I'm getting off because President Bush didn't do this, that or the other,' I would liked to have known from Magic: Well, what should the President have done that was not done. And I did not hear that from Magic."

How different, really, is life for Arthur Ashe and Magic Johnson, as opposed to some poor child in the inner city who has acquired AIDS?

"I would say a great deal different. I have suffered no negative reaction from anyone. I have kept all the cards and letters and telegrams that have come my way since my announcement, and there are literally no negative reactions at all.

"I do hear all the time, from various AIDS support groups and gay rights groups, that there are lots of people, gay and straight, who have problems because they are now publicly known to be HIV-positive or have ARC or have AIDS. They lose insurance, apartments, homes, jobs, family, friends. That's rather common in many cases."

What can the public really do?

"I'm glad you ask. I think the first thing we need to do, because of the sheer number of gays who make up the AIDS caseload, we literally need to separate the two issues (social and medical), if at all possible.

"Let's look at the AIDS issue medically and scientifically, and look at it in isolation (from the social) to see what can be done, because when you try to comingle the two, you really run into problems.

"Secondly, continuing on that thinking, PTA groups, boards of education, community boards, have to seriously consider things like condoms, and clean needles. Those are practical measures of containing the spread of AIDS."

When Jackie Robinson was dying, fighting diabetes in a very acute form late in life, Roger Kahn told him, "This is a cornball question, but in all the years you played ball, all the adversity, do you think it prepared you for this, dealing with your mortality?" And Jackie said, "Absolutely. It did prepare me, it allowed me to adjust, it made me more self-reliant." Could you talk about that, how you became more self-reliant through the ordeals of tennis as a young man?

"I would almost give the exact same answer. And let me quickly go through the similarities between Jackie and me. Both born in the South. Both went to California to make our mark. Both went to UCLA. Both were army officers. Both turned pro at the same age. Both had the same length of years as professional athlete, both had debilitating diseases at an age in life when you wouldn't expect it. So there are a lot of eerie parallels between Jackie and me.

"Having said that, tennis is different, in that it's an individual sport. You very much have to be self-reliant, whether you like it or not. And I do think a lot of that self-reliance, self-sufficiency, has enabled me to adjust very quickly to anything my doctor says—'Well, you have to do X, Y and Z, yesterday.' Well, fine, I can do it, just like that.

"Some other people say, 'Oh, no, you mean I've got to put a whole lifetime of habits and foods aside?' My attitude is, if I have to change, I change.

"Maybe that's why I'm what the medical doctors call a longterm AIDS survivor, because I've been able to adjust quickly."

Do you have a stronger commitment to humanity, do you feel maybe more than you ever have in your life that people are basically good?

"I think people are basically good, but the first law of nature is survival, and people will commit some acts that they would normally not think of doing if it's a matter of survival.

"There was a great TV show on the Donner Party. They had to resort to eating human flesh of others who did not survive. You do what you have to do to survive, and some people, as you say, quit, and some hang in there for longer periods of time.

"My difference, I think, is that my circle of friends have never been ones to waver. They were with me before and they're with me now."

There's the famous Bob Dylan song, "I Shall Be Released." Do you feel more liberated, knowing what you have known since 1988?

"Yes, that's a very good question. Not only liberation, but I have felt since I found out I had AIDS in September of 1988 that I am more creative, more productive, I've seen some connections, I've realized some insights that I may not have realized before.

"I also find out that this is not unusual for people who feel that they have less time left than they normally would have."

Arthur Ashe was not just a great competitor on the court; he took the best of what athletics has to offer and elevated it. He took the confrontation of a game and translated it into something far more important. He confronted the opponents of freedom and human dignity, and he scored an ace. His wars are over now, but for anyone who believes in what he believed in, who fights for what he fought for, the war rages on—without the able warrior, but still in need of soldiers who will fall into place and press on. Arthur Ashe was a magnificent human being, but as a husband and father he is irreplaceable in even more profound ways. For his wife Jeanne and daughter Camera, and for the millions who will never forget him, including me, he will always symbolize the best of humanity, courage, conviction, passion, the love of truth, honor and wisdom. In a life where he rarely had one, and in a sport that makes it mandatory to win, the phrase "Advantage, Ashe" seems oddly ironic. The world was at an advantage while he lived, and so much poorer with his passing.

FIVE

SHOWBIZ

People in show business have a saying that you should never follow an animal act. But for my money, the toughest act to follow is a war.

That bit of wisdom, which I will explain in a moment, is one of the things I've learned in twenty years or so of working in front of live audiences.

That's on my other job. A lot of people who see me on *Up Close* are unaware that I have another career, outside of TV: my night-club act, in which I do a wide range of impressions, tell some funny stories, and sing with videos that I have created from sports clips.

I've played big rooms in Las Vegas, nightclubs, conventions and banquets. I played the Grand Ole Opry with Loretta Lynn, and I've shared bills with everyone from John Fogerty to the Four Tops to Lou Rawls.

The stand-up act is something I work hard at. It's completely different from the work I do on television, and performing live can be enormously fulfilling. It can also be frightening. Like the night I stepped onto the stage and faced three thousand stunned pizza retailers.

In the winter of 1991 I was offered a nice gig, entertaining the members of the National Pizza Retailers Association at their convention in the New Orleans Superdome. I was on the bill with the Pointer Sisters and Pete Fountain, which is great company. I was the opening forty-five minutes.

It was the biggest live show I'd played at that point in my career. From backstage I looked out onto a sea of faces on the floor of the Superdome. The videos for my act would run on the giant Superdome TV screen, and my keyboard man, Marty Steele, would pump his amazing sounds through speakers the size of railroad boxcars. The atmosphere was like a big rock 'n' roll concert.

Timing is so important in show business. A few minutes before I was to go on, the public address announcer said to the gathering:

"Ladies and gentlemen, will you please find your seats. We have a special message from the President of the United States."

Because of the timing, just as the show was scheduled to begin, I think the general expectation was that this was going to be some kind of videotaped greeting from President Bush, thanking the conventioneers for the wonder of thirty-minute home-delivered pizza.

The President came on the huge video screen and a lot of the people applauded.

But this was no recording, it was a live TV announcement. The President greeted us solemnly, then explained that the United States and its allies had, moments before, launched Operation Desert Storm against Saddam Hussein. President Bush said that Allied forces were raining bombs on Iraq, ground forces were ready, and that many lives could be lost.

The audience was in absolute shock. You could hear gasps and murmers. I looked out from backstage and I saw eyes wide, mouths open.

As the President finished his message, the audience fell deathly quiet. The Superdome PA announcer waited about one beat and then, as the curtain went up, he said grandly, "Now, ladies and gentlemen! Welcome, please, the comedy of Mister Roy Firestone!"

Now the audience was really stunned. *Our nation has just gone to war and this idiot is going to stand up there and tell jokes?*

I couldn't walk out there and say, "Let's all go home, folks." I'm as patriotic as the next guy, but nothing would be served by calling off the show.

Thinking fast, I said, "Ladies and gentlemen, I just heard the announcement, too, and I'm not going to insult you by saying we're now going to have an evening of frolicking and levity. But I do know this: In our country, we're very honored and privileged to have the right to say and do as we feel, and this includes the performing arts.

"I would hope that tonight, in the spirit of democracy, we enjoy ourselves as best we can under the circumstances, with great love and reverence and prayers for our fighting men and women in Iraq.

"But first I would like to ask for a moment of your time, to sing this song."

I cued Marty and launched into "God Bless America." It was very eerie, with the profound silence of the audience and the booming echo of amplified sound in the Dome.

Even scarier, I suddenly realized I hadn't sung "God Bless America" since grade school, and I didn't remember all the words. Fortunately, the pizza folks began to stand and join in, and they carried me through.

It really was a stirring moment, and when the song was over there was a thunderous ovation—not for me, but for the song and for the country. Then I went into my act, and it has never gone better.

My parents were stunned when they found out that I was in show business.

Bernard Firestone, my dad, made the shocking discovery one night when he was sitting in his favorite chair in our living room in Miami. He was listening to the radio, to the Peppy Fields Show on the Mutual Broadcasting System.

Peppy Fields broadcast live from a Miami Beach hotel. Her show featured all sorts of vaudeville-type acts, which then abounded in the Miami area.

"Next up," Peppy told her radio audience, "we have a young man named Roy Firestone."

Bernard Firestone almost fell out of his chair. He had no idea that his fifteen-year-old son was an entertainer. He listened as I did my five minutes of impressions and singing.

When I got home that night, ten dollars richer, my dad's jaw was still hanging. He knew I was a ham, that I did impressions, but he thought it was just a goofing-off-around-the-house kind of schtick.

I started studying Sammy Davis Jr. and Jerry Lewis when I was about eight, and by fifth grade I was doing impressions of JFK. I got thrown out of my eighth grade English class one day for impersonating the teacher, Mrs. Elson.

But my folks had no clue I had taken my talents the next step, actually trying to break into the schmaltzy Miami Beach hotel circuit. I didn't tell my dad, because he was crazy about show business, knew everything about the great actors and performers, and I was afraid I would embarrass him with my little act.

My mother, to this very day, disapproves of my second career. She says, "I'd much prefer that you not be a clown." She pictures me with makeup, a red nose, and a hat with a squirting flower. She's deathly afraid I'll make a fool of myself.

So I launched that career secretly, at least until my dad heard me that night on the radio.

Not long after that, I put that career in mothballs for about ten years, until after I was established as a TV sports guy.

Then I slowly got back into it, and now "my act" is a big part of my life. I love it, but there are times when I think my mother was right.

Like the night I had to give Frank Sinatra the hook.

Because I truly am one of the great Frank Sinatra fans of all time, please let me say that I believe I caught The Chairman of the Board on a rare off-night.

Ever have nights when you're not as alert as you'd like to be, not at the top of your game, maybe under the weather or over-worked or jet-lagged? Sure you do. So do I. And so does Frank. The man does a million shows a year, sharp as a tack, command-ing the stage like Schwarzkopf commands an army. But Sinatra is human.

Anyway, this was 1989, and it was the biggest night of my

professional life. I was invited to share the stage with Old Blue Eyes at a huge Las Vegas banquet at Bally's–Las Vegas. I was to emcee the black-tie fund-raiser for the Barbara Sinatra Children's Center in Rancho Mirage, near Palm Springs.

The heart of the program was a roast of Tommy Lasorda, Sinatra's good pal. There were two thousand people in the audience, at a thousand dollars a plate, and it seemed like all two thousand were famous people. Gregory Peck was there, Rich Little, Red Buttons, sports people like Vin Scully, Harry Caray, Dave Stewart

An omen: Shirley Jones was to sing the National Anthem, but there was a mixup and her band didn't show. Fortunately, my keyboardist is a one-man band, and Marty was ready. He signaled that he would accompany Shirley. She started to sing, Marty hit his electronic keyboard, and there was no power.

Shirley sang a capella.

Next came what must have been a fifteen-course meal, a stupendous spread. Then it was showtime.

I got up, did an eight-minute intro and routine, a few impressions. I was nervous as hell but the audience was great and it went well.

Now it was time for me to bring on the man, Sinatra, and I introduced him with all the proper drama and respect. I noticed that Sinatra, as he walked up to the stage, was carrying one of those huge snifters which usually contain just a whiff of brandy. But Frank's drink looked like a Big Gulp from 7-Eleven.

Frank was not going to sing; just do some roasting of Lasorda, his longtime buddy. Since Sinatra is not a comedian, he had his eight or nine jokes typed on file cards, and the jokes were also scrolled on a TelePrompTer in front of the podium.

"I've known Tommy a long time," Frank said, delivering the first joke. "He's not the smartest guy I ever met. I don't think he can even spell ESPN."

It was cute, the audience laughed.

"Tommy comes from a tough neighborhood. His teacher asked him, 'What comes after a sentence?' Tommy said, 'An appeal.' "

Nice response. Frank finished the eight jokes. I looked at the Teleprompter. It flashed, THE END, and went blank.

But Frank was reading off his cards, and he shuffled the last joke to the back of the pile and said, "I've known Tommy a long time. He's not the smartest guy in the world . . ."

I was stunned. People were laughing, they figured Sinatra was doing a kind of parody of himself, like "Want me to run through these jokes again, folks?"

Then something terrifying happened. He finished the replay of Joke No. 1, flipped that card to the back of the pile and went right on to Joke No. 2. The laughter began to die out and people were rustling nervously.

At the head table just below me, Barbara Sinatra was waving at me to intervene. Gregory Peck was stage-whispering to me, "Roy, get him off!" Tom Driessen, one of Sinatra's best friends, was frantically signaling for me to stop this runaway train.

Here it was, the highlight of my show business career, and somehow I had to get Frank Sinatra off the stage, gracefully.

Jilly Rizzo, Frank's bodyguard (who has since passed away), was sitting behind me. I turned and whispered, "Jilly, what should I do?"

Jilly gave me an understanding look and, in a voice that sounded like it was coming out of a deep tunnel, told me, "Leave him the —— alone."

Boxing promoter Bob Arum was in the audience, and he had a plan. He was sitting with his fighter, Roberto Duran, and he told Duran to go up to Sinatra and do a bit of fight schtick. Fighters know they can always get a laugh by putting up their dukes like they're going to fight. You introduce a prizefighter to Mother Teresa and he'll make like he's going to clunk her on the chin.

Anyway, the idea was that maybe Duran could distract Sinatra, who by now was about to start his third run through the pile of jokes. Duran walked up behind Sinatra and tapped him on the shoulder. Sinatra turned, saw a short, dark-haired young man in a tux, and thought Duran was a busboy. He turned back around and said, "When we're finished with our dinner, they can take our plates, but right now I'm still speaking."

The place erupted in laughter, I jumped right in between them and said, "Ladies and gentlemen, Frank Sinatra and Roberto Duran in the old busboy routine! Funny stuff!"

Finally Frank sat down, and the show went on.

Joe DiMaggio was a tough audience. I performed at a banquet of the World Baseball Federation, an international group that promotes baseball, and The Yankee Clipper was in the front row, along with Mrs. Bart Giamatti, Mrs. Roberto Clemente and Sadahara Oh.

I'm certainly a big enough baseball fan to get goosebumps performing for Joe DiMaggio, but I noticed that Joltin' Joe didn't seem to be having the time of his life. Gradually, he warmed to the show, but I didn't get to him until the closing piece, a baseball video and a song called "I Used to Be a Brooklyn Dodger."

It's an emotional and poignant song, about growing old as much as about baseball, and DiMaggio seemed truly moved by the song and the video. When it was over, he was the first person on his feet, applauding.

I sang the same song at a show in North Carolina, and Mike Schmidt and his wife sat listening with tears streaming down their faces.

Reactions like that make the whole business worthwhile.

My first big Las Vegas gig was as the opening act for Lou Rawls at the Golden Nugget. Steve Wynn, who owns the hotel, had seen me do my stand-up and he hired me to co-headline with Rawls.

On opening night I felt an unbelievable amount of pressure and anxiety. It's strange to see your name six feet high on the big marquee. Every member of my family was in the audience, including my son Andy, who was eight months old then and looking sharp in his tux. Gale Sayers had heard I was playing Vegas and had flown in from Chicago just for the show.

I wanted to do well for myself, and my family, but I especially didn't want to mess up the show for Lou Rawls. The opening act is important for setting a tone for the evening.

Most people assume that the headline act chooses the opening act, endorses that act, hires that act. Often that's not true. In this case, Rawls and I had never met. He'd seen me on *Up Close*, claimed to be a fan of the show, but he knew nothing about what I did onstage.

Rawls introduced himself to me backstage just before I went on.

He said, "What are you gonna do tonight, my friend?"

I told him I was going to do my regular act. He looked surprised and said, "You've got an act?"

"Yeah, I do jokes, impressions, sing a little."

Lou said, "God bless ya, good luck to ya, I'll watch you here backstage on the monitor."

Some people who watched with Rawls said that during my act he started pacing around, saying, "This guy is good, man! What is going on! I never knew Roy Firestone did this!"

I got a standing ovation, and some headliners hate to see the opening act do that well, but Lou could not have been more gracious and congratulatory, that night and for the entire week. He even invited me to open for him in Atlantic City. I couldn't do it because of my TV show, but it was very flattering to be asked.

Another Las Vegas story:

I played a corporate job there in 1992, the day of the Tommy Hearns–Roberto Duran fight. I did the show in the afternoon, then went to the fight with a friend, Gary Miller, who is a TV comedy writer.

Duran was favored, but Hearns knocked him cold. Right after the fight I ran into Tommy's guys, including manager/trainer Emanuel Steward and they said, "Tommy would love it if you would come to his victory party. It's at midnight at the Maxim Hotel, fifteenth floor. Don't tell anyone else."

Gary and I had a few hours to kill before the party, so we went to dinner. I'm not a drinker at all, but I had a few this particular night, and Gary had several.

We were teetering around town, just enjoying the weirdness of Las Vegas, and about midnight we figured we'd head over to the party.

At the Maxim, we got off the elevator at the wrong floor and walked right into a huge Conga-line of some sort, a hundred Panamanian people dancing through the halls, singing and yelling.

It turned out to be Roberto Duran's party—his "Sure you got knocked out, but you fought like a lion" party. Roberto was wearing shades, singing the Panamanian national anthem. We fell in with that group for a while, then tore ourselves away to find the Hitman's victory party.

We got into the elevator. It stopped one floor up, the doors opened and there, in a group, stood Elvis, Janis Joplin, Buddy Holly, Jimi Hendrix, Jim Morrison, and Bobby Darin. All of whom, incidentally, had been dead for years.

It seems that the hotel's "Legends of Rock 'n' Roll" show, featuring these incredibly realistic impersonators, had just ended. The Legends were just out looking for a little fun.

Gary and I stared at the Legends. They stared back, and then, all at once, they shouted, "Roy Firestone!"

Then they got in.

"Where you guys goin'?" I asked, making small talk.

"Wherever you're going," they said.

I turned to Elvis and said, "What's your name?"

"Elvis," he said.

"But what's your real name?"

"Elvis. I'm the only Elvis impersonator who has legally changed his name. You know, there are a lot of Elvis impersonators, but I'm the only one named Elvis. I'm the real one."

They asked where we were headed and when we mentioned Tommy Hearns, they went nuts. They said they were so busy working that they never got to meet any celebrities. Gary and I decided to bring them along to the party. We weren't supposed to bring any additional guests, but we figured six dead rock 'n' roll legends didn't count.

Walking through the hallways trying to find the party, knocking on doors, we must have looked like an LSD version of *The Wizard of Oz*, with me as Dorothy.

We finally found the party, which wasn't quite as wild as the loser's consolation party.

I had forgotten that Hearns is one of the world's most dedicated Elvis fans. Huge fan. Collects all kinds of Elvis memorabilia.

We walked in and Hearns's eyes lit up.

"Elvis! Where you been?"

"You know, Tommy," Elvis said in his Memphis twang, "I'm sorry I couldn't come to the fight tonight, but I hear you did me proud."

"I did, Elvis. I won it for you!"

It was a truly touching moment. And people say there is no sentiment in Las Vegas.

I mentioned my keyboardist, Marty Steele. Marty does his work in the background, but he is a big part of the show, a musical genius. He can sit down at his synthesizer and within a half hour, put together a full arrangement that can sound like anything from Led Zeppelin to the Benny Goodman orchestra.

Marty is also the original wide-eyed innocent. He's bright guy, but not the most worldly. His first ride in a stretch limo was like a trip inside a UFO.

We played a big Nike banquet in Oregon. At dinner, Marty wound up seated next to Philip Knight, who owns Nike and is a billionaire, Howard Hughes kind of guy.

Marty: "Hi, I'm Marty. What's your name?"
Phil: "I'm Phil."
Marty: "Hi, Phil. What do you do?"
Phil: "Well, Marty, I run this place."
Marty: "Ahhh. Free shoes, eh?"
Phil (laughing): "Yeah, I guess so."
Marty: "Roy and I are getting free shoes, too, plus we're getting paid."

Marty and Phil wound up getting along famously. They seemed to have a great time talking. Why shouldn't they? They were both working a nifty scam to get free sneakers.

What I do can be very ego inflating, but it can also be the ultimate humbler. Sometimes a kind word from a person you respect goes a long way.

I got a letter about three years ago.

"Dear Roy:

My father once told me, 'When you see something you like, tell the person.' I'm telling you I see what you do (on TV) and I like it a lot. I'd love to get a chance to tell you in person, perhaps even be a guest on your show.

"Sincerely, Jerry Lewis."

The Jerry Lewis? Nahhh. Couldn't be. But the letter was on official-looking Jerry Lewis letterhead.

When I was about ten, Jerry Lewis and Sammy Davis Jr. were my inspiration. I don't delude myself that I am even in their universe, entertainment-wise, but those two never had a bigger admirer.

I was stunned at the letter. I called the phone number on the letterhead, and after a couple weeks of phone tag, I reached Jerry and we had a long talk. For me, this was like Tommy Hearns meeting Elvis, only Jerry Lewis was real.

He invited me to his house. It turns out he's a huge sports fan, he likes to bet on games now and then, and he's nuts about playing golf and racquetball. He's also a collector of memorabilia— a Lou Gehrig glove, Ben Hogan's clubs, Sam Snead's putter, a Gil Hodges glove.

He agreed to be a guest on *Up Close,* to talk sports, and he wound up doing two shows. After one of the shows I mentioned to Jerry that I have a nightclub act, and that I was about to open in Las Vegas. He asked me to send him a video of the Las Vegas show, and I did.

Not long after that, when I was slugging through a rough day, my confidence shot, the phone rang and it was Jerry Lewis. He gave me a twenty-five-minute critique of my act, most of it extraordinarily flattering.

He said, "Roy, you do all your impressions and then at the end of the act you say, 'I'd like to sing a song in my own voice, if that's okay.' Don't you *ever* apologize for performing. Don't you ever ask permission. If you're doing well, you've got their permission. If you're dying, get off.

"Do what you feel you should do in your life, enjoy what you're doing, and don't ever apologize."

Now, when I hear the occasional comment, "Who does Firestone think he is—a talk show guy or a comedian? Can't he make up his mind?" I replay in my head what Jerry Lewis told me.

And then there is Bernard Firestone. I mentioned earlier that my father was very leery of me getting into this end of show business. He was proud that I was successful in my "straight" TV job, and he felt that messing around with comedy or a stage show might undercut my credibility. He reasoned that an allegedly serious TV journalist shouldn't be seen in public impersonating Johnny Mathis.

I felt I could effectively work both careers, and so in 1981 I started working comedy clubs around Los Angeles.

One night, not long into my new standup career, I played the Improv in Hollywood. Dad and Mom came to watch. I felt good about the material, but the audience didn't. I couldn't buy a laugh that night.

I was fairly devastated. Maybe I should rethink this stand-up career.

As I was walking outside with my folks, my mom said, "I told you this would happen."

But Bernard said, "Lousy audience, kid. I thought you were great."

That was the proudest I've ever been as a performer.

SIX

MOUTHS THAT ROARED

Everything you've ever heard about Howard Cosell, good and bad, is true. But it's probably understated.

Like the time he barfed on Don Meredith's cowboy boots in the Monday Night Football announcing booth.

The story was that Cosell lost his lunch on Dandy Don's boots prior to a game at Franklin Field in Philadelphia, apparently due to a slight overconsumption of alcohol. Meredith assured me that the story is absolutely true.

However! (as Howard would say), what wasn't reported is that the floor of the announcing booth was a steel mesh (Meredith tells me), and the booth was suspended over the grandstands.

So Cosell barfed not only on his partner's boots, but on the heads of dozens of fans.

That'll ruin your popcorn.

Still, that's only one side of Cosell. I would be remiss to write him off as an overserved, overbearing buffoon. The man was very important in my life, as a teacher. From him I learned what I wanted to be in this business and what I *didn't* want to be. He was my two-way role model.

When I started in sports, Howard Cosell was my absolute hero.

He was an original in a business of copycats. He was courageous, a pioneer. No matter how many boots he barfs on, you can't deny him his due as a giant in sports broadcast journalism.

I met Howard at the 1978 World Series in Los Angeles, where I was working as a weekend TV sports anchor. Before one of the games at Dodger Stadium I was in the dugout with Al Michaels and Jim Palmer, and I happened to be doing my Howard Cosell impersonation. Just then Cosell walked onto the field near us.

Naturally, Michaels and Palmer called him over. They introduced me to Howard, then sat him down on the bench and told me to do some more of my impression.

Based on what I had seen of Cosell on television, his delightful interviews with Muhammad Ali and such, I had an image of him as a man with a great sense of humor. I was partially right.

He does not, however, find humor in Howard Cosell impersonations. He seemed neither amused nor flattered at my version of him. In fact, he seemed somewhat annoyed, rolling his eyes as if to say, "Great, what's next on the bill? Singing dogs?"

Then I dropped the Cosell and did my Keith Jackson impression. Howard found it hysterical. He broke up. A friendship was formed.

For the next year and a half, Howard sort of took me under his wing, a very informal apprenticeship. He would phone me from New York once a month or so to ask my opinions or offer advice.

"Roy! Howard Cosell. Let me ask you a question. What do you think of the situation as it exists now in Cincinnati?"

Cosell had a TV show, and he asked me to come on as a guest, do some comedy and impressions. He especially liked my spoof of an *Evita*-style Broadway musical, "Fernando!" "Don't Cry for Me, Tom Lasorda," etc.

I flew to New York to do the show and spent a little time with Cosell. We would be standing on a streetcorner waiting for a cab and he would do play-by-play of the street action. If Howard's awake, he's on.

Cosell had to fly to Los Angeles, so we were on the same flight west. So were actor Robert Wagner and Los Angeles mayor Tom Bradley.

As the plane started to taxi for takeoff, Howard said very loudly, "Start spreading the news!"

Not singing, understand. Talking, but loudly.

I said, "When are you leaving, Howard?"

"I'm leaving to-*day!*"

"What do you want, Howard?"

"I want to be a part of it!"

"Where?"

"In old *New York!*"

It's amazing, but he did the whole song that way, with me doing the setups. It's even more amazing that none of the passengers jumped out the door.

Cosell appointed himself emcee of the flight. Five minutes after takeoff Howard shouted across the first-class cabin to Robert Wagner.

"R.J., come over here! Tell me what's going on with your career at this juncture, as we speak! With the great Natalie Wood. Jill St. John, you and I both know what's going on there, *and!* Stephanie Powers, the lovely and luscious . . ."

Several times during the flight Howard called Wagner over to our seats—"R.J.! Get over here!"—and I assumed they were old pals, drinking buddies. At one point I asked Wagner how long he had known Cosell.

"About twenty minutes," Wagner said.

Then Cosell would summon Bradley, who is a quiet and dignified man.

"Thomas! Tommy!"

It may have been the first time in Bradley's life he was called either of those nicknames.

"Tommy, come over here! You know I made your political career, you know it was MY doing that established yourself as one of the great black leaders of the twentieth century. Don't become an Uncle Tom like so many repute you to be. Be proud!"

Fortunately, Bradley and Wagner were good sports, and we made it to Los Angeles with no fights or arrests.

I was doing my ESPN interview show by then and I kept trying to get Cosell on as a guest, but he kept declining. Finally he agreed to be on the show.

"All right, Roy, I'll do your show," he said in his Cosellian condescension. "I don't want to, really, I have no interest in doing your program, it does me no service. You understand, of course, that virtually no one watches your show! The audience is minimal, but my contributions will be considerable.''

And so on. But he did the show.

It's a talk show, but of course Howard doesn't talk, he lectures. Cosell at his best might be described as compelling bombast, and the show went well.

By then we had developed what I assumed was a sort of friendship. Every time Cosell came to Los Angeles he would phone me and tell me to meet him for lunch at the El Padrino Room at the Beverly Wilshire Hotel.

There, Howard would hold court in a manner I've not seen before or since. From his table, he would broadcast the lunch for the entire room.

"There's Tova Borgnine. Wife! Of actor Ernest Borgnine. Who! In 1955 scored an Academy Award for the motion picture *Marty. Tova!* Leave your husband and come with me. Your lower lip is quivering with excitement. The electricity is palpable. Just imagine being in my carnal grip.''

It was an amazing show, and as it went on and on, Howard got louder and more Howard-like.

There was a piano bar and Cosell loved to sing, although, as I mentioned, he didn't actually sing. He *talked* a song, in the same voice and manner he used to analyze a defensive alignment on Monday Night Football.

"It was *Laura!* All alone in a wonderous land . . .''

Every time a waitress would come within ten feet, Howard would flirt, although I'm not sure "flirt" is the word I'm looking for.

"Come with me and I'll have you weeping and moaning!" he would say as the waitress put down another drink. "There will be no room for any further ecstasy in your life. They'll have to peel you from the ceiling, because, in point of fact, I will have sexually satisfied you in ways you could *never imagine!*''

The waitresses, thank God, knew how to handle this kind of act, so Cosell never got what he deserved—a pitcher of ice water dumped on his head.

He was nonstop. He had an opinion of everyone, and every opinion was negative. People he hated, he ripped; people he liked, he ripped to show his affection. A name would be mentioned and Howard would be off.

"Joe Jones? Why, the man was a virtual fraud! Over*rated!*"

No person was so great that his achievements and accomplishments couldn't be caustically berated and belittled by Cosell. But it was unbelievably funny.

A waitress would bring him another cocktail and instantly, in midsentence, he would shift his attention to her.

"What's your name, my dear?"

"Patrice."

"Patrice! A lovely name! Patrice, in a few moments, I'll have your clothes completely off. *And then!* I'll show you an evening of sexual passion you'll not soon forget."

The deeper he was into lunch, the more colorful his fantasy play-by-play.

"What is your brassiere size, my dear?"

The Howard Cosell show. Singing, zinging, sexually harassing, like the juggler keeping three plates spinning at once. Smoking, drinking, hacking his smoker's hack, laughing his machine-gun laugh. Crazy and amazing.

Bob Uecker told me about a time he and Howard worked a baseball game together in Los Angeles. Somehow Howard had upset the fans in Milwaukee by making a derogatory reference on the air about the team or the city, and now he was under siege. He had even received a death threat, by mail or phone.

After the game Uecker and Cosell passed a spirited evening in the lounge of the Beverly Wilshire. Howard spit in the eyes of his Milwaukee critics, telling Uecker, "Nothing will deter me from saying what needs to be said!"

At closing time, Uecker carried him upstairs to his room, dumped him on his bed, and left.

But just outside the room, Uecker decided it would be fun to bang on Cosell's door.

Cosell: "Who's there?"

Uecker (disguising his voice): "Cosell, we're going to kill you for the things you said about the Brewers."

Cosell (screaming): "My God, I'm being assassinated!"

The next morning Uecker was in the coffee shop when Cosell dragged himself downstairs, groggy, his suit rumpled and his toupee tilted at a dangerous angle.

He sat down with Uecker and said solemnly, "You know, Bob, at two o'clock this morning there was an attempt on my life."

Uecker strung Howard along for a few minutes, then said, "These assassins, Howard, did they mention something about the Brewers?"

"Yes! How did you know?"

"Because it was me, Howard. I was the assassins."

Howard did not laugh.

I talked Howard into making a second appearance on the show, and it proved the undoing of our beautiful friendship.

He had just written a new book pompously titled *What's Wrong With Sports*, in which he trashed every friend or associate he ever had in the broadcast business.

He attacked O.J. Simpson and Don Meredith, killed Frank Gifford. Anyone who ever spoke into a mike, Cosell murdered in this book. The book should have been called *Cheap Shots at Former Pals*.

I decided to question him on the issue of loyalty. On the show I asked him why he had written so negatively about so many of his associates and alleged friends.

Cosell bristled at the question, said haughtily that he would never let friendship stand in the way of telling the truth. As if national security was threatened unless he revealed his opinion of what a lousy announcer Gifford is.

He remained in a testy mood, and near the end of the show the discussion swung around to baseball and the beauty of the game. He said challengingly, "What beauty do you see in it?"

Is there no romance to the game, in your mind, Howard?

"Well, what is the romance in *your* mind?"

The fact that two teams . . .

"Is the romance lodged in a Pittsburgh courthouse? Is it lodged in a player coming out of that courthouse, where under grant of immunity he testifies that he snorted cocaine, even during the action, but he comes back to New York and at Shea Stadium, before 52,000-plus people, they stand and give him an ovation, and three miles away, across the river, 55,000-plus people sit and boo the Canadian national anthem?"

But that's not the quality of the game of baseball, Howard.

"*But that's* what's happening in America and the game of baseball today, and things are out of whack when that's done! And it's up to somebody in the United States to talk about things like that, to do things, and to stop romantically ignoring everything that's wrong, because until people like you, who have a forum, wherever it is, get on the bandwagon and expose the wrongdoing, that's the only way you can improve sports, and *then* concentrate on what you deem to be, and have every right to deem to be, esoterically beautiful!"

When he was finished I felt like I was guilty of covering up Watergate.

After the sign-off Cosell told me, "That's it! Our friendship is over. I'll not do your show again, and I'll not want to see you again."

And he has kept his word.

I found it ironic. Howard's style was to be the prodder and the challenger, yet put in the role of challengee, he blew like a volcano.

That show depressed me. I felt like maybe I'd let Cosell get in too many punches without countering. A couple of days later I was at a fight, and I ran into Al Michaels and TV boxing analyst Alex Wallau. Michael said, "What a great show the other night with Cosell!"

I said, "Yeah, very funny, Al."

He said, "No, I'm serious."

I said, "How can you guys look at that as a great show?"

Al said, "Because it revealed Cosell. It showed what he is—how sad and angry and joyless and humorless he really is. And how his Don Quixote thing with the windmills of life has turned him into, not just a lone voice in the wilderness, but an angry voice."

I want to stress how much I had admired Cosell. At the same time, what I really learned from him in the end was how *not* to be bitter, detached, alienated.

In Billy Crystal's movie, *Mr. Saturday Night,* Billy's character says to his brother, "I made you, I did everything for you, I brought you up from nothing. See how terrific I did? See how brilliant my work was? You owe me the respect and admiration and applause."

This could have been Cosell's speech to everyone he knew.

In the movie, the brother countered with one line: "Yeah, but you could've been nicer."

Howard deserves respect for taking chances and risks, for being a tenacious lion of a reporter, a journalism groundbreaker who, once upon a time, even had a sense of humor.

But he belittled waitresses and fans and associates and friends.

He could've been nicer.

From the dark side of the moon, into the sunshine. From Cosell to Tommy Lasorda. Not that Tommy is perfect. He can be pouty and grumpy, scream at reporters, typical baseball-manager stuff.

But Lasorda likes people. He likes almost everyone. He is an absolute, incurable ham who will give an entertaining speech to any group of people—"group" being one or more persons.

Before any given Dodger game you can pass a lively half hour in Lasorda's spacious Dodger Stadium office. Ask him about his fan mail, he'll haul out a cardboard box of fan letters (he personally answers thousands a year), tear one open, read it, maybe pick up the phone and call the sender.

"Hello, is this Helen Johnson? This is Tom Lasorda. I wanted to thank you for your letter . . ."

Or get Lasorda going on a topic like, "Tell me about your major league career (twenty-six games pitched, zero wins)."

The rap is longer than the career. The Dodgers called him up from their Montreal triple-A team in 1954, then sat him on the bench. Take it away, Tommy:

"Ten, twelve days and I ain't even f—— warmed up in the bullpen! We're in Milwaukee, we win the first game of a double-header. I'm takin' a leak between games and Zim [infielder Don Zimmer] comes in, says, 'You won't believe what I just overheard.' 'What?' 'No, no, I better not tell you, you'll get pissed.' 'Tell me!' 'Okay, I overheard [Dodger manager] Walt [Alston] talking to [pitching coach Ted] Lyons. Ted said, 'Who do you want in the bullpen for the second game? Let me bring Lasorda down.' And Walt said, 'No way. Since Lasorda's been here, we've got more life on the bench than we've had in years.'

"I make a beeline for Walt's office. I'm screaming at him, 'Did you bring me up here to be a cheerleader?' "

The story goes on. Tommy finally got into his first big-league game, threw a wild pitch and had his leg slashed covering home plate. It took four Dodgers to restrain him from going back out and bleeding to death on the mound.

It turns out Alston was right. Tommy was and is the greatest cheerleader baseball ever had. When God was passing out energy, Lasorda thought it was the cafeteria line and went back for thirds.

I took a limo ride once with Tommy, going to one of his gigs. He'd been making the winter rounds, two and three speeches a day, and he was running out of gas. He finally deflated like a balloon, became very quiet, almost depressed and sullen.

"Oh, Christ I'm tired, Roy. I tell ya, I gotta get some rest. I can't keep goin' like this."

Then we arrived, the limo door opened and there was a small crowd to greet him. It was as if someone had turned on the spotlight and handed Tommy a top hat and cane.

"Howya doin'? Out-standing! You a Dodger fan, pal?"

Don Sutton and others have attacked Lasorda, some of them on my show, for being a phony and a bad manager. But some of that is simply baseball. When Abe Lincoln made that speech about not pleasing all of the people all of the time, I think he was referring to a baseball manager dealing with twenty-five princely, neurotic, wealthy ballplayers.

One thing about the great talkers of sport is that they polarize public opinion. It's Charles Barkley's 50-50 rule: Half will love you, half will hate you.

I can tell you from being around Lasorda at public appearances, the love is real. He is a famous sports figure who talks to people, who looks them in the eye and makes them feel he really cares about them.

He has a phenomenal memory for names and faces and events and anecdotes.

But because he is outgoing and famous, and on the field he can be combative and profane, he has his detractors. To them he represents the phoniness and loudness of L.A. and Hollywood.

But his feelings are real. Tommy suffered a huge personal tragedy in 1991 when his only son, Tom Jr., died at the age of thirty-three. "Spunky," as everyone called him, seemed so vastly different from his old man that a lot of people, I think, assumed that they were not close. For years Spunky lived in the Hollywood nightclub-glitter subculture, a strange little world a million miles from baseball.

Yet Tommy and Spunky were very close. They frequently got together for lunch or to visit, and Tommy was always proud of his son. The death hit him hard. He came on the show a few months later and talked about it.

I asked him how he had managed to maintain his enthusiasm for baseball in the immediate wake of his son's death.

"When I sign my contract with the Los Angeles Dodgers," he said, "I've got a commitment and a responsibility to give them everything that I have within me. When I walk through that clubhouse door, no matter how dejected or depressed I might feel, I must put on a new face, an enthusiastic face, a winning face, because if I walk in dejected, depressed and down, that's gonna be the attitude and atmosphere of the club."

Did you ever say to yourself, ''What more could I have done?''

"No, because I felt that Jo [Tommy's wife] and I and our daughter, we gave him all the love, we did everything we could for him, we loved him very, very dearly.

"I told Jo, and I said this to my mother when my father died, I said, 'Jo, if you and I could have seen God and he said, 'I'm going to give you a son, but you're only going to be able to keep him for thirty-three years,' what would you have said, Jo?' She said, 'I would have taken him.' I said, 'That's exactly what we've done.' "

I mentioned Charles Barkley's 50-50 rule. Barkley, however, wouldn't care if it was a 1-99 rule—one percent loving him and 99 percent throwing stones. He would still be Charles.

Sure, he often feels he is misunderstood and unjustly criticized.

He is the only person in history to claim to be misquoted in his own autobiography ("I should've read it," he lamented). But I'm pretty sure Barkley has never lost sleep worrying about his Q rating. He has a Zen-like attitude about saying what's on his mind, and it is a crowded and creative mind.

"I think I have an obligation to myself and to God to tell the truth," Charles told me. "Whether people take it good or bad, that's not my worry. I feel that if you can look yourself in the mirror and honestly feel like you're telling the truth, I think that's all that should matter to you . . . I think people should say to themselves, 'Is Charles telling the truth?' instead of worrying about who it offends."

But what about discretion, Charles?

"Well, I feel better when I say what I think. I don't want to go out one night and kill myself 'cause I'm so upset inside. I got to let it out."

One characteristic of all the mouths that roared is that they are ultracompetitive, beyond the normal intensity of great competitors. They all lose lousy. A lot of Barkley's controversies have come about because of this absolute need to win.

He became the focal point of the All-Star Game two years in a row, complaining about playing time. He still holds a deep grudge against Bobby Knight for cutting him from the 1984 Olympic team. He hated losing in Philadelphia so badly that he made himself obnoxious to teammates and the front office so they would be forced to trade him.

"God gave a lot of players in the NBA talent," he said. "I don't want to be like them. I want to be a step above."

An insensitive, arrogant person? In some ways he is, but if you're really sneaky you can catch Barkley visiting children's hospitals when there are no camera crews around, doing nice, human things.

An elderly lady phoned a Philadelphia radio show to complain about Barkley's behavior. He got her phone number, invited her to a game, picked her up in a limo, was her "date" for the evening.

"I just wanted her to know that the mean, aggressive guy who's on the court, who only wants to win, is not the same person off the court . . . I told her point blank, 'Listen, I'm not going to change the way I am on the floor, 'cause the main thing is winning. I'm going to be nasty, aggressive. I'm going to try to intimidate, I'm going to try and do anything I can to win. But I just want you to know I'm not like that off the court.' She was very nice."

Barkley told me of an incident on an airplane, shortly after he came on the show and discussed his "I'm the Nineties nigger" comment.

A flight attendant handed him a note from another passenger. The note said, and I'm paraphrasing, "I never liked you, but I play golf at an all-white country club. I saw your TV interview the other night, and for the first time in my life I realized that whether I like you or not is not important. I'm reexamining why it is I go to this all-white club, why I shut out a whole class and culture of people just because I have something they don't. I'm going to quit the club, although I still don't like you."

Charles was very proud of that note.

What is it about basketball coaches that makes them the best talkers? Maybe it's that their profession demands, above all, salesmanship. They have to sell themselves to prospective recruits and then to fans and alumni and the press, over and over, day after day, almost door-to-door.

Or maybe it's just that the basic freewheeling nature of the sport attracts the wilder personalities.

Two of my favorite college coaches are Abe Lemons, who has stopped coaching but hasn't stopped talking, and Rick Majerus, who will never stop doing either.

Abe, when he coached, was one of those animated types. Liked to keep the officials alert by engaging them in conversation.

Abe told me, "Everybody says, 'Why is he acting like that?' Put yourself in my place. You see your life going down the drain, and the referee is out there blowing the whistle on you.

"One ref, I said to him, 'Can you give me a technical for what I'm thinkin'?' He said, 'No.' I said, 'Well then, I'm thinkin' you're an SOB.'

"There used to be a referee named Charley McCarthy. He shows up one night, he makes a bad call, I said, 'You know, I liked you better when you had Edgar Bergen with you.' And the guy gave me a T. And he showed up the next year and he's wearing a toupee. And I said, 'Charley, I still know ya, and you're the same sorry guy,' and he says, 'That'll be a T.' "

Tell us about the time there was a rumor going around that you had died, Abe.

"I'd gone to Detroit to do a speech. I got up to my hotel room and the phone rang. It was [Detroit columnist] Joe Falls. He said, 'We have a report that you've been killed in an auto accident.'

"And I denied it. I said, 'One of the reasons I know I'm not dead, you don't go to Dee-troit when you die.'

"Someone called my nephew and he called my wife, said, 'You heard from Abe?' She said, 'No, why? Is he hurt?' He said, 'No, he's dead.'

"Then I called my wife. She had mixed emotions."

Abe's wife is a philosopher in her own right.

"Tark's a nice fella," Abe said of much maligned Jerry Tarkanian. "I think he's one of the great coaches. My wife summed him up, she said, 'He just *looks* like he did it.' "

Abe, how about the low graduation rates of athletes?

"If they let me teach class, I'd graduate 'em all. Alabama coach Wimp Sanderson had the best answer. Someone said, 'How many guys you graduate?' Wimp says, 'Everyone that wants to.'

"During the Korean War, nobody flunked out. I'd say my graduation rate at Oklahoma City and Pan American was 100 percent. You flunk out, you go to war. Now you just go to another school. If you're a good player, you can go to fifteen schools."

Abe is part Indian.

"I had five Indians on the team at one time. We put 'em in a basket-weaving class. They got the curve so high, the white guys flunked out."

Rick Majerus lives in a motel on the Utah campus, carries a basketball around in his car and looks for pickup games, and I guess you could say he doesn't take himself too seriously.

"I resemble the economy," he said. "My hair's in recession, my waist is in inflation and it causes me to have a big depression."

It's not that Rick doesn't want to be a sex symbol, it's just that people won't let him.

"I was in Cincinnati," he said, "staying at the Stouffer Hotel, and I was recovering from my heart surgery. Paul McCartney and his band were in town for a concert the next night at Riverfront. They were staying at the same hotel, they had the entire top two floors.

"So I get up to jog in the morning, around ten o'clock, a beautiful late February day, and there's about two thousand people milling around outside of the Stouffer, waiting to get a glimpse of McCartney or someone in his band.

"I'm walking out the door, a little boy, a nine-year-old who'd been in my basketball camp sees me and bolts underneath the police line, comes up and says, 'Can I have your autograph?' Now all of a sudden these two thousand people go crazy, they all think they've hit on a celebrity.

"People are chasing me, coming at me from every direction trying to get autographs. Somebody in back yells out, 'Who is it? Who is it?' And a guy says, 'It's one of the Stooges.' And another guy says, 'No, it's Uncle Fester from the Addams Family.' "

Tell us about Salt Lake City, Rick.

"I call it the land time forgot. It's a throwback to the Fifties. It's like Milwaukee in the Fifties and Sixties when I grew up. It's mostly Mormons, and the rest of the people in Utah, I think, are under the Federal Witness Protection Program. You see a restaurant, Giovanni's, up the canyon, twelve miles from nothing, you know that this guy told on someone sometime in his life."

Speaking of restaurants, you love to eat, there's no secret there.

"I've had seven heart bypasses. I tell people I've had one for every major food group."

Rick's genius, obviously, is in recruiting, but he says it's never easy.

"I was recruiting Walter Watts, he was 6' 6" and 323. First time I saw Walter, he had on a yellow polo shirt with blue-piped striping. I thought Saturn was approaching.

"Another time, I'm recruiting this Mormon boy who lives in rural Utah. He's a great player and we get down to the decision-making day and he says, 'Coach, I'm going to go to BYU.'

"I said, 'Why?' He says, 'Because I spoke to God.' I said, 'You mean you prayed on it?' He said, 'No, no, I spoke to God.'

"I said, 'Let me get this straight. God spoke to you and told you to go to BYU?' He said 'Yeah.' I said, 'Son, let me tell you something, I've had Jesuit priests on the end of my bench for twenty-five years, guys who have converted people in Africa. You're talking about your Mormon mission, these guys are on a *major* mission. Poverty, chastity, and obedience for life. And *they* never saw God.'

"I said, 'I gotta tell you something, son. I'm so frustrated, I'm turning God in to the NCAA. This is an illegal recruiting violation. He's an alumnus, he had no business talking to you.'"

SEVEN

PHILOSOPHERS AND BEATNIKS

I read about an art teacher in Kansas City who gave his students an assignment to answer the question, "After all these years, what is it that you know?"

The only rule was that the answer or answers had to begin with the phrase, "I know that . . ."

I thought it would be an interesting question to spring on a guest some time, but not just any guest. I didn't want to get answers like "I know that good pitching always beats good hitting, and vice versa," or "I know that I got screwed on my last contract, man."

But when Willie "Pops" Stargell was on the show, I had a hunch that this was a pitch he could drive.

Willie can go deep. He went deep 475 times in his twenty-one-year big league career. And he tends to take a deeper look at life than most athletes with whom I've come in contact. So I explained the assignment to Willie and I asked him, "After all you've done and seen, what is it that you know?"

"Not a heck of a lot," he said, laughing.

Then he took a breath and, in his big, deep voice, spun an answer that was pure poetry.

"I know that prayer brings peace," he said.

"I know that hard work brings just rewards.

"I know that respect creates gentlemen.

"I know that on a cold winter morning in Pittsburgh, I enjoy a good bottle of Korbel Brut champagne with the Sunday papers.

"I know that good friends and good things will keep b.s. away.

"I know that hitting a baseball, especially a home run, is like a runaway freight train and your first time you have sex—somewhere in between.

"I know that rubbin' shoulders with good people, not great people, is a real joy.

"I know that I know what I don't know."

Wow. Now you have an inkling of why Pops Stargell has a special place in the hearts of the fans and media who got to know him.

Stargell is one of those rare people who stop to smell the pine tar. Listen to him talk about baseball:

"Every time the umpire said, 'Play ball,' I took it literally, that he meant to just go out as we did when we were on the sandlots, get dirty, have fun and get mad when the sun goes down. When we were kids, we really didn't know what the score was a lot of times, but we had an awful lot of fun.

"And then a guy comes along and says, 'Do you want to play baseball?' I said, 'Well, I've *always* played baseball,' and he said, 'Well, we gonna *pay* you. We gonna teach you how to play better, gonna let you travel around the world, rub shoulders with fine people, and if you do well, we'll pay you more.'

"Well, I've always felt that the guy was crazy. And then learning how to win, given that pleasure, yeah, it turned into nothing but a joy.

"Thinkin' back on the championship years, from 1970 to 1980 we were in six divisional playoffs and two World Series. We intermingled with the Phillies and the Cincinnati Reds, who we felt were just great competition, not only on the field, but you had a chance to study the individuals' characters, what they were all about.

"And when I retired, I went to a lot of those guys and told them what a pleasure it was to not only compete with them, but to have the pleasure of knowing what kind of people they were."

Stargell hit some long homers. He is the only man ever to hit a ball out of Dodger Stadium, and he did it twice.

You love to hit a baseball.

"I like to hit the ball hard. I wasn't trying to intimidate anyone, but it reminded me of the days when I was in the projects, hitting stones with a stick, over the railroad track, and I used to envision hitting home runs in a major league park.

"Once I got to the big leagues, it was a real joy trying to figure out how to hit that ball and get the good part of the wood on it, and just literally crush it, especially when it counted."

I'm a pushover for the philosophers, the guys who aren't afraid to talk about what they think and what they feel, to venture off the beaten path of sports talk. It's a rare gift, and I treasure the visits of a Pops Stargell or an Al McGuire.

You know who Al McGuire is, right? He's Holden Caulfield's favorite uncle.

When McGuire was coaching at Marquette in the 1970s, he once said, "I like seashells and balloons, ribbons and medals, bare feet and wet grass. Coaching is just a passing fancy for me. I hang around people who know nothing about sports. The guy driving a bus doesn't take a bus out on his day off."

McGuire was coaching his team toward a national championship in 1977 when fellow coach Abe Lemons dropped into a Marquette practice. Here's what Abe claims he saw:

"Butch Lee was layin' at the free throw line with his leg on the ball. Al walks in and says, 'What time do we practice?' Butch says, 'I thought you'd know, you're the coach.' Al says, 'Well, come get me when everyone gets here.'

"So they're going through practice. The first team's got two red shirts, a blue shirt, two green shirts. They argue with each other, Al hollers and Bernard Toone says, 'You're drivin' me crazy, Al, quit hollerin' at me!' Al says, 'Not until you do what I want.'

"He gets in a rasslin' match with one of his players. It's kind of a circus, but they won the whole shootin' match. I watched [Notre Dame's] Digger [Phelps] in practice. They got practice uniforms that's all the same. He blows the whistle and everyone knows where to go. They got beat in the first round."

Al never really was a coach in a normal, formal sense, and yet, fifteen years after he retired from coaching, he's more a coach than ever. I'm not sure what McGuire is, and I'm not sure he's sure, either, but I know he's working hard on finding out.

He is funny, yes, but that's a tiny part of Al McGuire. He's also wistful, thoughtful, curious. He is an observer, who also knows he is a leader. "Outside of my family, that's the most important thing to me, to be called 'coach'," he said. "I always wanted to be called coach. Of course, I'm no threat to anyone now, I'm retired fifteen years, but it's something I always wanted to do. I always wanted to sit in the front of the bus, 'cause the coach sits in the front of the bus.

"Being a coach is something that's respectful, and it's something that there's no price tag on. In just the last fifteen years, because of the boob tube, the dollars have come, and you get your share, but most guys that I know of did not go into coaching for the dollars.

"People don't like to hear this, but coaches are not intelligent people. If they were intelligent they wouldn't go into coaching, because it's too difficult to become the head coach. The real wackos are the football coaches, because there's about fifteen of them on every squad, and to get up there is so difficult."

Al feels he has a pretty good grasp on exactly what a coach is.

"In my third year at Marquette University, I had a ballplayer get in trouble. I always left my telephone number at the police station, so they called me and I went down.

"First of all, when your children or your friends get in problems, never ask 'em why. You're an idiot if you do. First thing you do is solve the problem, then a week later you punch 'em in the nose. But first you solve the problem.

"So I go down there and I solve the problem, and we're walking out of this police station, and the kid says to me, 'Gimmie a lift back to the dormitory, coach.' I said, 'Call one of your friends, big shot.' He said, 'I don't have a dime.'

"Didn't have a dime! Not an exciting story, but a story to think about. It shows you what a coach is. You're developing people.

You take care of your part of the bargain, which is to get them degrees, to improve their station in life, and to be close with them. And that's it, without a phony love affair, without a phony pattin' 'em on the back and so on.

"Bein' honest with 'em. And that's why there's not a ballplayer, a ref or a coach that I cannot look in the eye after twenty-five years of coaching. The greatest compliment I ever got in my life was when, after I retired, my mother called me and said, 'Al, I'm so pleased you left clean.' "

One of your quotes is, ''We rush for the stars as we crawl toward our graves.'' Explain that for us, would you?

"We gotta live on two planes. One plane, you've got to let your hair grow and put on the beach shoes and live in the moment—wet grass, bare feet, that type of stuff.

"A certain amount of pain is happiness, and as you go to those goals, you must also be aware that you're here for just a certain amount of time, and what I'm trying to tell people is to milk the day. Milk it.

"I feel like I'm eatin' breakfast every twenty minutes, the day goes by so fast. That's not good, but it is good, that means that you're having a good time."

You're a loner, right?
"Yep. Absolutely."

You've said you find more philosophy in a donut shop than anywhere else.

"Roy, that's like saying you're in love, it sounds so phony. Someone says, 'Are you happy?' 'Oh, I'm happy, I'm happy.' And it all seems phony, and I don't want to sound phony to your audience, but I just enjoy the touching. I enjoy garage sales, I enjoy sawdust, I enjoy a can of beer, a ham sandwich, my motor bike.

"But if anybody's with you, watching you, it's like an act, they think you're acting. I've gone by that stage. Matter of fact, Roy, I don't know when I'm acting and not acting. All I know is that it's been a beautiful roll. I've been rolling tens the hard way, and fours, and it's been a thirty-five-year hot hand.

"And as it ends now with television, it's like I'm taking a wheel-barrow over to the cashier's window. Not dollars, but the ride, the joy, the soul and the Dick Enbergs and the Billy Packers and Costases and Criquis and Joneses and Marv Alberts of the world. And to me it's just something that's precious, being called coach."

How do you feel about being inducted into the Basketball Hall of Fame?
"I didn't belong in it. I was so pleased when I got in it. I didn't realize it was such a moment. It was just something that I'm thankful for, but I still don't think I belong in it, I think I got in it because of the TV. I only had a decade of good coaching."

Let me throw some quick ideas at you, and you respond. The Seventy-seven national championship.
"If I would'a known crying meant so much, I would'a cried ten years earlier. That crying on the bench in Seventy-seven, Roy, changed me from surly, obnoxious, and arrogant to one of the boys. It made me another person."

You cry a lot. I noticed your eyes tearing up several times today. You're a very emotional person.
"It could also be that I'm winding down, I'm in the stretch of my life and so I'm just happy to be on this side of the grass."

I'm guessing there are not many football coaches who would tell this kind of story about themselves on national television:
Bill Walsh was talking about his final season with the 49ers, 1988, and what it was like just before the Super Bowl.
"When I stepped on the field in Miami, by myself, I broke down," Walsh said. "It was in front of fifty or sixty thousand people, but they couldn't tell, only I could tell. It was because of the emotion of the moment, the preparation. A lot of times you come unraveled a little bit emotionally, it's a result of a lot of other things—weariness, fatigue, you're drained and there's not much left to do but to show emotion."

Bill Walsh actually expected people to laugh when he announced in 1992 that he was leaving his lucrative, cushy TV football announcing job to go back to Stanford University as the head coach, at age sixty.

Of course, nobody laughed. The philosophers are bright guys, but sometimes out of touch with how people feel about them.

People don't laugh at Bill Walsh. He took a crummy San Francisco 49ers team and front office and turned it into what may have been, for one glorious decade, the ultimate football organization.

Then, when it looked like he might return to the 49ers in an advisory capacity in 1992, Walsh suddenly decided he wanted to go back to Stanford, where he had been head coach fourteen years earlier.

Unusual career move. Unusual man. He came on the show after the 1992 Stanford regular season in which he proved he is, if not a savior, at least still a football genius. Stanford routed Notre Dame at South Bend, and had its first ten-win season since 1940.

Walsh is a serious man. He is concerned, and not just about winning football games. He really feels like he's a teacher, that he has ideas and energy to contribute, and ultimately that's what Bill Walsh is about.

We began by talking about the personal effect a coach can have on college players.

"You really have an impact," he said. "I looked back, after taking the Stanford job the second time, at some of the photographs that were autographed by my former players to me. Beautiful things they said to me for having coached them, so I know I had a major impact on their lives.

"So you do, in a sense, formulate feelings and values and direction at the college level. And the guys are innocent, Roy. By and large they're innocent, and the forces that work on the professional athlete, from all angles, make it difficult for him to be rational and objective. But in college you can be, and are."

You have a lot of concerns, a lot of compassion for what's going on in the inner city. James Stockdale, you became good friends with him recently. He said, ''Bill Walsh should be appointed to a commission to look into the problems of the inner cities, that's how plugged-in he is.'' Give me some observations of what you think is wrong and what's happening in the inner cities, because you warned two weeks before the riots that there would be an explosion.

"Well, it's very simple. Our educational system has broken down totally. I don't blame the teachers. The public at large, the citizens of the state of California and the United States, are not interested enough in education, or feel so far removed from it that they don't care.

"You've got to go into the inner cities and make the schools the bastion of making sense, and for character and education, and for values, the American dream. You double the maintenance people, you double security people, you double the number of teachers. We pour our energies into it.

"Will it work right away? Not necessarily. There'll be some antagonism. But these bastions of education can be open virtually all day. Adult education at night, the entire year. Sports activities, drama, music, a cultural center in the inner city. And often directed by people from the inner city. But we need to pour our energies and our attention and our cash into these areas. If we don't, it will get worse and worse.

"There are too many forces at work on youngsters, too much asked of the teachers, and we just won't give it our attention. I was very, very, very disappointed in our former President Bush, not attacking this as everyone thought he would. I'm hoping that Bill Clinton will, I'm hoping that the people of California will, because something has to be done."

What about everyone wresting control of their own lives? Some say if they are manipulated, it's because they want to be, or allow themselves to be.

"Well, it's by degree. I think a person at college age, seventeen and eighteen, is not a totally mature, rational person, they don't have any wisdom and they don't have any experiences. They depend on what other people tell them and what very minuscule amount of experience they've had. They can make mistakes, they can misunderstand the dynamics of situations.

"When someone comes to their home and says, 'You're going

to get an education,' they never totally understand how much work they're going to have to put in. It may be that they think, 'Well, someone's going to hand me a piece of paper and I'm educated.'

"A good friend of mine's youngster is enrolled at one of the great universities. She had a little less than a three-point average, one thousand on the SATs, they told her she'd have to go to summer school and take two classes before she could be enrolled at the university. You think they're gonna do that with an athlete? They're not about to tell the athlete with much lower scores, much poorer grades, to go to summer school first. They know some other school would say, 'No way you have to do that.'

"I think progress toward graduation is vital. The course of study is vital. You have people fully prepared. We can't convince a person they're fully prepared when they're not. They may enter into the mainstream of the curriculum and they can't do the work. I say, if they ask summer school of the typical student, why not ask an athlete to participate as well?

"On the other hand, Roy, the aid offered these athletes is totally inadequate, it's an insult. You have a youngster travel two thousand miles to a university and you can't help him get back and forth to home. They have such a small stipend to live on, and that is compounding itself. First they feel inadequate intellectually, and secondly they feel inadequate because they can't participate in the natural things going on around campus."

How much did you feel the manipulator, part of this process?
"Well, Stanford's so unique, I can talk pretty bravely about it because there are not these kinds of things that occur there. It's one of the very few schools where this is true. All you have to do is move around in the San Francisco Bay area or the West Coast or anywhere, and you see these happenings.

"But an athlete expected to live on a minimal amount of money can't have a job because of the NCAA regulations, not a penny in their pocket, and feeling inadequate intellectually because they've been conditioned that way, they're expected to go out and practice three and four hours a day, at the sacrifice of their schooling. This whole combination forces them to be mercenaries."

This word has been used to describe you: are you aloof?

"Aloof with certain groups of people. I tend to meditate a lot, drift into thought a lot, and I can look indifferent to what someone has said because my mind's already moved on to something else."

Are you vain?

"Not to the extent that so many people in public life are, so many athletes and other coaches. I couldn't put myself in a category of a number of them, no."

Manipulative?

"In a sense. I worked with Al Davis. There's just a little strain of getting what you actually need. No harm done to anyone, but you do calculate some, no question about it. But not manipulative in the sense of a car salesman or something, no."

Insecure?

"Probably, if anything has driven me over the years, it may be insecurity. Feeling I wasn't quite up to it, having to work harder than other people, and feeling less gifted, in a sense, than many others. But that's the kind of thing that can push you over the top. So certainly, some insecurity."

Did you have a love-hate relationship with [49ers' owner] Eddie DeBartolo?

"We're two very strong, independent people. He comes from one arena, I come from another. We got along beautifully throughout the ten years in many, many ways. But Eddie has a lot of pride and definitely wanted success. We'd give him success, then he would be frustrated when there wasn't more.

"When your team loses key games, there's always a suspicion that there may be a better coach out there somewhere. This is a natural phenomenon. But I have to say again—Joe Montana–Bill Walsh, Ed DeBartolo–Bill Walsh, the best combination owner-coach, or quarterback-coach, there's been in the Eighties, and maybe ever."

Jim Finks said it's always been Bill Walsh against the world— that is Bill Walsh's genius.

"Well it is, in a sense. And it certainly has been utilized by our team [the 49ers] and nurtured and developed among our team. That's why they're winning now. It was us against the world, throughout.

"If one coach or one player were to step out, we'd close ranks and keep going. I can recall every time Joe Montana would be injured, not able to play, his replacement—Matt Cavanaugh, Jeff Kemp—would do just as well. Bill Walsh out, George Seifert in. Close ranks and keep going. So that philosophy has been the key to our success, and conceivably it is inbred in me."

If there's a common theme among the philosophers, it's an intense and overriding need to find out what life has to offer, and to go get it, now. It's not a desperation as much as it is a hyperenthusiasm, a capacity to see the possibilities where others see impossibilities.

Jim Valvano, Jimmy V, on the surface is a funny guy, a comedian. Great quotes, great enthusiasm. I never met a guy who enjoys life more. Sadly, he lost the coaching job he loved so much at North Carolina State over a scandal, and in 1992 he learned he has cancer.

But he's not hiding out. I ran into Valvano late in 1992 at UNLV, where Rollie Massimino was kicking off his first season coaching there with one of those midnight madness publicity galas.

Valvano was there with Mike Fratello and Tom Lasorda, and he gave a speech during the festivities.

He talked about life in terms of having a limited number of opportunities to suit up. He said he's had a lot of great thrills, along with all the adversity, and he has come to realize that every day he wakes up and puts his feet on the ground, he tells himself, "Let's go. Let's suit up again."

Because of his enthusiasm and humor and depth, Valvano is as good a guest as I've ever had on the show. Really a world-class talker.

"Nobody's bigger than the game," he said on the show a couple years ago. "The game is what it's all about. For me, it's vast, I'm in awe of it. We won a national championship, right? Still, there's not a gym I can walk into without wanting to go over and take a shot. Gotta take a J. I have a pretty good J, by the way.

"I love the game. You know what my biggest thrill is? Biggest thrill is at North Carolina State, down in the locker room before the first game of the season, I just gave my Knute Rockne speech No. 52, which I tell the kids is for me. I worked 365 days a year for thirty years and people say, 'Be calm.' How could I be calm? This is it for me, babe.

"I give a heck of a talk, I dive on the floor. The kids go up, and then I hear the band play the fight song, and then, just before tipoff, I go up and I just stand there and look out at twelve thousand people, and the cheerleaders doing backflips, kids out there swaying, and I'm in heaven.

"That, to me, is what it's all about. It's the moment and the atmosphere surrounding the game. Nobody's bigger than that. I can leave tomorrow and somebody else comes in and he stands in that locker room. I feel privileged to be part of college sport."

What about the recruiting?

"It's very hard. Say I'm recruiting you. I'm in your home and I say, 'What are you interested in studying?' You tell me, 'Anthropology.' 'Anthropology! We have the best anthropology program in the country. I was just playing handball with the chairman of the Anthropology Department!'

"And that's what it becomes, because of the tremendous pressure to win, because you're selling."

What about the academic integrity issue?

"I'll tell you a story about a kid named Lester George, at Iona College when I coached there. Lester's from Brooklyn. And he had a freshman year that was horrible, academically. I'm talkin' horrible. Should he have come to school? Should he be there?

"Lester is a beautiful kid, Lester wanted an education very badly, Lester should have had that opportunity. Sport helped him get that chance.

"End of his second year, I'm in my office one day, there's a knock at the door, it's Lester. 'I just wanted to tell you, coach— Lester George is going to be a junior.' He not only made it through, he now works for IBM in Manhattan, very successful.

You tellin' me he shouldn't have that chance?

"Let's be honest about the role sports plays in this society. Everyone wants to talk about how it's not that important. Maybe it's not, but by the same token, take a look around you. The sports pages, this show, the NCAA tournament—there's an awful lot of people who pay attention to it.

"Let's not be hypocritical. The fact is that colleges around the country do accept student-athletes who are somewhat below the standard of admission. However, the obligation of that school is to make sure they are given the opportunity.

"The sin is when the coach puts basketball before the youngster's education. We don't do that, and the majority of them don't do that. But it's a challenge, and I'm lookin' for all the Lester Georges of the world."

Tell us about your childhood, growing up in Queens.

"Everybody should grow up in a neighborhood where you gotta make up games. Where you gotta play Johnny-on-a-pony, kick-the-can, stickball. We got kids today, unless you drive them somewhere, and it's organized, and it's got Joe's Drug Store on the back of the shirt, they can't play.

"I used to get up in the morning and we'd go to the park and play. That's it. Play. We came back, my father used to say to me, 'Did you have fun?' I love that. You go to games today and the moms and dads sit in chairs and yell at the ump. I'm not against Little League. It's just that we sometimes lose the joy and fun of sport. I think when the game is over, you're supposed to be happy at the effort."

Would you have been the same person if you had grown up in Missouri?

"We're all products of our environment. I grew up in Queens, New York, with family all around—my uncles, my cousins. Everybody ate two o'clock on Sunday, we all went in and had a little pasta. Everybody had a mustache where I grew up.

"Then we move out to Long Island, I meet a little kid named Rusty. I thought that was a condition. I said 'What's your name?' He said, 'Rusty.' I said, 'Your name's gotta be Anthony.' So I'm an awful lot of where I grew up.

"When I got to Raleigh, they were shocked that I'd never been fishing. I said, 'How do you fly-cast into a fire hydrant?' "

(We showed a clip of Valvano's North Carolina State team winning the national championship in 1983, beating Houston. After the final shot, Jim runs onto the court like a madman.)

"This is one of those moments when people thought that I had lost my mind. All the other coaches win the national championship, they button their coat, they go shake hands with their opponent. This guy goes out of his tree.

"You gotta picture what was goin' through my head. I'm down in the locker room before the game. I get a nervous stomach before games. So I visited the little boy's room. This is a big game. And right before the game, a fellow from the NCAA comes in and says, 'Coach, good luck. I think you'd like to know, if you win this game you'll become one of only twenty-nine coaches in the history of the game to have won the national championship.'

"So I said 'Wow,' I get a little more nervous. Went right back into the little boy's room. I come out, a fellow from CBS comes, says, 'It appears that this game will be the most watched game in the history of televised basketball.' I said, 'How many people are watching?' He said, 'About fifty million.'

"I'm kind of emotional to begin with, so when that shot left Dereck Whittenburg's hand (an airball that was grabbed by Lorenzo Charles and dunked for the game-winner), I could see it's short. Now most people don't know this, but I did not want to play Houston in overtime. Most people don't know that I didn't want to play them in *regulation* time.

"All of a sudden Lorenzo Charles grabs it and dunks it. At that moment, what did I know? Two things. I had the ring. And fifty million people are watching. Big moment. Great chance to do something spectacular. So I'm gonna do something great. I'm gonna sprint out.

"Why? Because all my life I had grown up watching *Wide World of Sports*—remember what the agony of defeat was? The skier. But the joy of victory, they don't have one. I was gonna give 'em one.

"I would go out there and hug one of my players, especially Whittenburg, because Whittenburg for nine games in a row had hugged me. So what happens? I sprint out there at this great moment and Dereck Whittenburg, for the first time, he's hugging Sidney Lowe. I have nobody to hug. An Italian kid from Queens, New York, all by himself out there. I felt the joy of victory and the agony of defeat, all at once!"

You don't get the credit you deserve as a serious coach because you're such a showman.

"I'm glad you brought it up, because it is something I'm very sensitive to, something I can never understand. In this business, as in all businesses, they label you. If you are studious, your legs crossed, three-piece suits, you have glasses, you don't laugh that much, you're considered to be an X-and-O man.

"Or you can be a recruiter. And you can be a personality or a character. You're not allowed to be funny and also serious. I am serious, but I don't take what I do seriously. The kids who play for me, I want them to understand that someday the cheering stops.

"You don't get introduced every day. They're not going to say, 'Now, here he comes, starting at left desk, give him a hand!' "

Tell the story about why Cozell McQueen, a South Carolina kid, wanted to go to North Carolina State.

"I gotta preface this by saying I love Co. But. Everybody told me you're not supposed to recruit down there. The kids are gonna stay in South Carolina. I said to Co, 'Why'd you finally decide to come to N.C. State? He said, 'Coach, I wanted to get out of the South.' "

When all is said and done, what do you want to be remembered for?

"All right, this is it: I read about Lila Acheson Wallace, I think she's the co-founder of *Reader's Digest*. In her will she wrote, 'Being of sound mind and strong body, I spent it.'

"And I think that's what I want. When it's all over, not the money, but the whole thing—the energy, the life, and the love for life. I want it all spent. When it's all done, I want you to be able to say, 'His dance card was filled.' "

EIGHT

THE BAD
AND THE
UGLY

One fascinating aspect of doing the show for so many years is watching people grow and change. Over a period of a decade or less, a regular guest on the show will go through what amounts to an athletic lifetime, birth to death and if they're lucky, life *after* athletic death.

Mike Tyson's seven-year lifetime flashed quickly and dramatically in his visits to the show. He first came on when he was nineteen, and it was difficult to interview him. Emotionally, he seemed about twelve years old. He was painfully shy and soft-spoken, almost frightened, and his answers were short and guarded.

He was a young man completely opposite from the man who was so commanding, almost snarling, in the ring. The raging bull, in a suit and in front of a camera, was like a kid whom you wanted to buy an ice cream cone.

He cringed at any comparison to a great fighter.

"I don't even belong in the same category as a Muhammad Ali," he once told me. "I'm not worthy to be in the same room with him, to be talked about in the same sentence."

That kind of respect is rare, but the young Tyson was a rare guy.

There was a sweetness to him, a humbleness.

Looking at that first show, it's hard to believe that within seven years, this kid with so much apparent potential as an athlete and a person would be beaten up, in the ring and in life, that he would be angry, bitter, manipulated, paranoid, spiritually adrift, and, finally, tossed in the slammer, from whence he had come less than a decade before.

Through the years you could see the evolution of Tyson just by watching his prefight press conferences. The tone went from shy, to cordial, to grotesque—Mike cursing at reporters, falling asleep, berating and ridiculing opponents with homosexual taunts.

Still, almost until the end, until the rape trial in 1992, I remained a Tyson fan. I rooted for him to make it. He was on the show six different times over the years, and his growth was remarkable. His confidence grew, his presence, his maturity. We became, I felt, good friends.

When things were going well, I remember thinking what a sensational TV fight analyst Tyson would make. He can really talk the game.

"Meldrick Taylor, Roy, is showing me a lot of the way it was with Battling Johnson in 1908, Johnson being a man with a disproportionate number of punches thrown, not significantly a defensive fighter, but very much a parallel to the way it was in the very first fight."

The ex-Brooklyn street punk suddenly sounded like Wilfrid Sheed. His language was flowing, graceful, no hesitation, great command, confidence, vocabulary.

"People have a tendency to look at Sugar Ray Leonard and say he has a lot of similarities to Sugar Ray Robinson. Nothing could be further from the truth. In 1956, when Sugar Ray fought for the middleweight title against Joey Maxim . . ."

Whoa! Mike expounding on the theory of boxing relativity. The light was on. He was a true student of the sport, and spoke in intelligent, measured terms.

I have never met an athlete with as much reverence for his sport, as strong a grasp of its history. In an age when young baseball sluggers have never heard of Mickey Mantle, Tyson's knowledge of boxing honored the sport, made him an even more worthy champion.

Then it started to unravel. Roger Kahn, writing about Billy Martin, applied a quote from the novelist Turgenev to Martin: He couldn't simplify himself. And that's the way it was with Tyson. Fighting, and talking about boxing, he was in control. Everything else, forget it.

Boxing was his glue, the thing that kept him whole. He could have been a great trainer or manager, or TV man, after retiring.

But the most elemental fighter of his generation—no socks, no robe, no h.s., let's fight—got hit too hard and too fast with being champion.

A lot of people, once outside their element, lose their ethic, their discipline, their focus. Their life purpose becomes muddied. And there's probably nothing that will assault your sanity and your focus and your whole being like becoming heavyweight champion of the world when you're barely out of puberty.

"Inside the ring," Tyson once told me, "I'm totally in control of the situation. You're in control in the ring. It's something you've prepared for, your training, months and months, and it's like a diagram, everything's written out in your head that you've planned to do. Outside, the ring, it's the unexpected so constantly. You don't know what's going to happen day by day."

Tyson, alone, had a chance. Team him up with a Robin Givens and a Ruth Roper, a Don King, a sycophantic entourage, a billion dollars, and the whole deal starts to get very shaky.

Not that Tyson ever had what you would call a solid foundation. His father skipped out on the family before Mike could remember. His mother worked, was never around, and then died of cancer.

His one father figure, Cus D'Amato, schooled Tyson as a fighter but skipped a lot of fundamental educational necessities, then died when Mike was still a teenager. Cus was all heart, but his influence over Mike was too limited and too brief, then he was out on his own again.

For a while Tyson could pull it off. He was still winning fights, and he could overcome a lot of his public relations disasters by falling back on his youth and innocence and charm, and the power of his title.

I don't remember ever seeing a boxer crumble in the ring like Tyson did against Buster Douglas in Tokyo in 1990. Tyson came on the show after that fight and I asked him, "Is it true that you were relieved to lose the title?"

"Yes," he said. "You watch television and they say as soon as you lose, they [leeches and hounds and reporters] all disappear and leave you alone. And I said, 'Good, now I can relax, now it will be cool.' But it wasn't that way. It was totally different."

That blows my mind, Mike. You're a guy that lived to be the champion. The Marciano record and all that! And you were relieved to lose the title?

"You got to understand what I'm saying. It gave me a chance to recoup, because of my situation at the time, my life was under a microscope, basically. And unfortunately, nothing changed."

By that time it was clear that Tyson didn't know who the hell to trust. He had dumped his manager, Bill Cayton, and he had fired several former pals, including trainer Kevin Rooney.

"You don't know the situation with Bill Cayton," Tyson told me. "And just because I got involved with Don King and he put me aware to—we got proof how Bill Cayton stole money, how he put it into a corporation."

Okay, forget about Bill Cayton for a second.

"No, you can't forget about Cayton, because it's a fact that's what he did."

What about Steve Lott?

"I never did anything to Steve Lott!"

You fired him.

"He was the enemy. He chose who he'd rather be with."

How about Kevin?

"Kevin was with the enemy as well. You're either with me or against me. If you're not with me, you're against me, so you can't be around me."

He had become Fort Tyson, under siege. The same insecurities that fueled his fury in the ring were messing up his life. I don't think Mike ever really believed in himself. I think he was built up to believe in himself by Cus. Like "I'm the baddest dude in the world."

That was real, but it was from Cus. Then Mike surrounded himself with this entourage of butt-kissers, the John Hornes and Rory Holloways, people who could tell him how great he was but who couldn't do anything for his soul.

The women, the jewelry, the cars, all those things were supposed to be his symbols of great success, but they were symbols of desperation.

Nobody knows what would have happened to Tyson had Don King not joined the party. Not that all the blame for Tyson's major fall can be laid at King's feet, but anyone who tries to tell me Don King didn't hasten the collapse will always get an argument from me.

Isn't it sad that for the last four or five years, it has been impossible to discuss Tyson, as a fighter or otherwise, without also discussing Don King? It's almost as if King attached himself to Tyson, like a 250-pound tapeworm in a tux.

Do I blame King for Tyson being in prison? Certainly not. Mike is responsible for his own misguided actions, including the crime of rape, and including the hiring of Don King.

But when Mike Tyson walks out of prison, and a certain somebody is there to greet him, wide smile and hand out, I hope Tyson has become strong enough to keep on walking.

Tyson signed with King in 1988. And even though King essentially lured Tyson away from Cayton by convincing Mike that these white people were trying to steal his manhood and money, to control him, that's basically the role King assumed.

Tyson loved New York City, but almost immediately he moved to Cleveland, near King's home. Tyson's attorney for the rape trial, Vincent Fuller, is also King's attorney.

Yet Mike tried to convince himself that King was setting him free.

I asked Tyson if, in hooking up with King, he was trying to rediscover what he called the "sense of direction" he had when he lived with D'Amato.

"No, I'm independent of myself now," Mike said in an unintentional bit of insight. "Basically I'm not lookin' for anyone to lay my head on his shoulder or anything. Basically, after goin' through all the turmoil (of the failed marriage), I'm just really unhappy with myself, and I don't need a psychiatrist, there's nothing wrong with me, I'm just feeling totally magnificent."

Talk about your mixed messages.

I mentioned to him something that Sylvester Stallone once said, that the big problem with being wildly successful is that suddenly there's nobody to tell you "no" anymore, no one to cross-examine you. I asked Tyson if there was anyone around who could do that for him.

"Well, basically I have advisers. I have Don King and I have other friends who are very objective, and I listen to their opinions, and when it comes down to it, I do basically what I want to do. Sometimes you make the whole assessment and go about it in your own way, make your own decisions."

What is Don King's role?

"He's mostly my promoter. I want him to be my promoter and my adviser, and I made that decision after going through a great deal of difficulty, calling him up . . . I basically believe I don't need anybody."

And yet King was always around.

I'll tell you a story that I think says something about King and his need for control over Tyson and everyone else.

In 1989 I was asked to write and produce a one-hour TV special on Tyson, "Portrait of the People's Champion," for syndication. I was to have full access to Tyson and, I thought, control over the creative content of the show.

Tyson was great. Cooperative, friendly, open, honest, fun. There were some great moments. Kenny Rogers, the singer, agreed to work on the special as a still photographer, and he took some wonderful pictures and got along great with Tyson.

Rogers is a very unassuming superstar. One day when we were filming on location, Kenny drove the equipment truck. It was lunchtime so we pulled into a McDonald's drive-thru and Rogers ordered for the whole crew.

When Kenny drove up to the window, the guy at the counter looked at him and started to say something.

"I know what you're gonna say," Kenny said. "Kenny Rogers, right? I can't stand that guy anymore. People tell me I look just like him."

"Yeah," the kid said, "you sound just like him, too."

Rogers shook his head sadly.

Anyway, he and Tyson hit it off famously. At first they were in awe of one another, then they loosened up and got to be good friends. They spent a lot of time together, talking about life, childhood, whatever.

So the filming went well. Everything was smooth. To a point. In a part of the program we had some footage of Tyson in earlier times. One clip was of Mike wearing a T-shirt on which was printed ROBIN AND MIKE. Even though that marriage hadn't worked out, it was still a significant part of Tyson's life story.

King stepped in and said the ROBIN AND MIKE on the T-shirt had to go. To erase it from the footage, we had to use a machine called a color corrector. The machine and labor cost about $30,000, which I'm sure came out of Mike's pocket, but we erased Robin's memory.

When the project was nearing completion, but before the final editing, King told me, "We don't want nothin' negative."

I was surprised. King knew that the show, overall, was a flattering look at Tyson. I said, "What do you mean, Don? I have to talk about Mike's past."

He said, "You're not gonna talk about nothin' in the past, you're only gonna talk about the positive."

I had assumed King was always around simply because he was afraid to let Tyson out of his sight. Then I discovered that King was the executive producer of the show, and had approval over the content.

It was too late for me to back out of the project. I had put too much work into it and I was committed, ethically and professionally. But I took my name completely off the credits. Even though the show was still basically good and won several awards, was nominated for an Emmy, I was glad to be disassociated with what turned out to be a Kingscam.

Covering up Tyson's human blemishes was not enough for King, and here's vintage Don. We had interviewed several celebrities talking about Tyson—Chevy Chase, Sinatra, Arsenio Hall, Eddie Murphy—and their tributes fit in nicely.

But late in production, I got a fax from Guber-Peters, the distributors of the program, informing me that we had to redo that portion of the show. There wasn't enough good stuff about Don King.

I phoned the higher-ups to protest.

"The name of the show," I reminded them, "is 'Portrait of a People's Champion.' It's not a tribute to Don King."

I was told, "Do you want to be the producer or not?"

I said, "I think so, but how far do I have to go?"

This far: We had to send crews out to reshoot the celebrities, and this time ask them why Don King is a great American. We had to get Donald Trump, Jack Kemp, people like that talking about Don King's wonderfulness.

His self-aggrandizement, of course, spoke loudly for itself.

But at least King is a wacky, zany, comical guy, right?

You bet. That's the hook he uses to reel in suckers like me. Early on, I bought into that routine—the funny hair and the wild jewelry, the big words and malaprops, the wild cackle.

For a newspaper columnist or a TV sports guy looking for a fifteen-second sound bite to spice up an otherwise boring day, Don King was great. You get sucked into that backslapping persona, you forget your responsibility to probe beneath the surface.

Then you start to see the dark side, the exploited fighters, the manipulation of the sport, the deviousness. And all of a sudden that crazy laugh becomes scary.

I'll tell you who Don King is. He is the Joker. I think he would make a hell of an archvillain for the next Batman movie, a cross between the Joker and the Riddler, with the crazy laugh and the rhyming, fractured wordplay.

Like the Joker, behind King's grin is a rage, an anger. King, remember, killed a man.

Still, the fight game is full of creeps and thugs and leeches. What makes King stand out is that he uses racism as a tool to manipulate black fighters. He convinces a Tyson that he is being ripped off by whitey, then King himself, according to ample testimony, picks his fighter's pocket while he's got his protective arm around him.

Here's King, the protector of the black boxer, quoted in a story in *Vanity Fair*, talking about how he wishes he could have arranged a Tyson-Holyfield fight before the rape trial: "I would have captured immortality in the promotion. Plus, Mike woulda went to jail a rich man, you know what I mean? And I'd have had some money, too, while he was gone."

During Tyson's rape trial, I gave a commentary on the show, expressing my disappointment in Tyson for even allowing himself to be in this situation, whether or not he was guilty. I quoted the old line from *On the Waterfront,* where Brando says, "I coulda had class, I coulda been a contendah, I coulda been somebody, but I'm Just a bum."

Not long after that I ran into King and he launched into me.

"Firestone, you are out of line! You continue to repudiate and eradicate all of the things that Don King has done . . ."

And so on.

I listened, then I told him, "I'm sure I'll have you on the show again sometime, because you are a force in boxing, but don't think for a second that I am going to buy your b.s. about only-in-America and the flag."

And I did have him on the show again, because I don't believe in censoring my guest list based on personal grudges. I think it's important to let people like King come on and have America see them and judge for themselves.

Generally I'm not a combative, confrontational type of interviewer, but I make an exception with King. During one heated exchange I said, *You called Evander Holyfield a nigger recently.*

"Is he? Tell me the truth, now, you tell me that he isn't?"

No, I don't think he's a nigger. I think he's a black man who . . . Do you think that it's because of white guilt that I'm not saying it?

"Everybody has their opinion, but the only constant has been nigger. Throughout four hundred years! So now, you got to understand if you're going to make him white, that's great, 'cause I may think he is, too. Maybe he's my color, but not my kind."

You said, ''Big business spits on the name of Holyfield. The people who like him, like him because he's docile, because he can be controlled—Run, Johnny; sing, Johnny; dance, Johnny.''

"Is that incorrect?"

I think so. You don't think he has dignity?

"He may have, [but he] don't utilize it, he never demonstrates it. He lets guys do duplicitous, treacherous, egregious things to him and he just goes right along, always a smile, an altar boy or candle boy. He stand for nothing, so he don't live for nothing."

So you're saying he's an Uncle Tom?

"You finding all the right names, I have to agree with you, Roy, because he wants to be less objectionable and more acceptable."

I don't claim to always know what the hell King is talking about. An example of his convoluted rhetoric came when I asked him about his repeated use of the word "nigger." I pointed out that Richard Pryor once said that this word perpetuates a wretchedness.

Why? Why use that word?

"I think it's fundamentally necessary to use that word, because that word strips you naked from all type of facetiousness and pretense, and when a person is dealing with you, you can deal with what is real and pragmatic and realistic, not trying to deal to make you like me, to understand me. Blacks must learn to extrapate being less objectionable and more acceptable."

You call yourself a nigger?

"Ab-so-lutely. Ain't no question. I'm not going to give you any equivocation. As you know, the stereotyped image of us in America is that we're lazy, we're lethargic, we're slothful, we can't rise to the occasion, you know how we lie and all of us steal. With an appraisalship like that, it's needless to get out of bed!"

The point, exactly? You got me. All I know is that whenever I see King coming—or hear him coming, since you always hear him before you see him—my instinct is to flash the Batman alert signal into the skies over Gotham City.

NINE

SUPERSTARS AND ODD COUPLES

I was working in my office at *Up Close* and the phone rang.
"Hello."

"Hello, is this *Up Close?*"

"Yes, it is. Who's this?"

"My name is Wayne."

"What can I do for you, Wayne?"

"Who am I speaking to?"

"This is Roy Firestone."

"Oh, Roy! Listen, did you ever have Mark Messier on your show?"

"No, I haven't. I know he's a great player, but I'm not sure what kind of clamor there is to have Mark Messier on the show."

"Well, he's in town and I could bring him over. I'd really like to see him on the show. He's a great guy and he really doesn't get enough publicity. He should be MVP this year. I could drive him over."

I said, "Who the hell *is* this?"

"It's Wayne."

"Wayne who?"

"Gretzky."

I laughed. I thought the voice sounded familiar.

"Would you like to come on, too?" I asked him.

"I would do it, Roy, but to tell you the truth, I'd just love to see Mess on the show, see him get some public recognition. You don't even have to send your limo."

That should tell you something about Wayne Gretzky.

He is probably as unimpressed with himself, as unaffected by massive fame, as any huge superstar I've ever dealt with.

Sportswriter Rick Reilly was working with Gretzky on his autobiography and they decided to go to dinner at Spago, L.A.'s ultrahip pizza joint.

Reilly let Wayne make the reservation, figuring "Gretzky" might have more maitre d' appeal at Spago than "Reilly."

Gretzky phoned.

"Hello. Would it be possible to get a table at eight thirty tonight? . . . Oh, you have nothing before ten? Oh, Okay. Thanks anyway."

Reilly was aghast.

"You didn't tell them who you are!"

Gretzky shrugged and said, "I can't do that."

Clearly a man who will never make it in Los Angeles.

It's a Gretzky quirk, his stubborn refusal to be anything more than he is: a guy who plays hockey.

And that's what makes him unusual. The people at the very top, the ultrasuperstars, are all special or eccentric, each in his or her own way.

Wilt Chamberlain kind of summed it all up one day on the show when he was talking about Bill Walton. Wilt said, "Bill Walton had a definite aroma about him."

I think "aura" is what Wilt meant, but maybe not. The very special athletes all have the sweet smell of incredible success.

The aroma manifests itself in many ways.

Gretzky, for example, has more rituals than the Catholic Church. He refers to them as "routines," but they are not routine. I'm not sure he would even admit all of them, because the ones he admits paint a strange enough picture.

A partial list: He won't get his hair cut on the road, he tucks one corner of his game jersey into his pants, in warmups he always shoots his first shot wide left, he dresses for each game exactly the same way, and his pregame eating habits make Wade Boggs's chicken mania look normal.

At the arena, Gretzky drinks a Diet Coke, then a glass of ice water, then Gatorade, then another Diet Coke, then Gatorade, then he eats four hot dogs.

And it must be in that order?

"Pretty much. I just believe that I have to have a full stomach to play properly."

Isn't there something about keeping your sticks separate from the others?

"My hockey sticks, I don't like them touching other sticks, and I don't like them crossing one another, and I kind of have them hidden in the corner. I put baby powder on the ends. I think it's essentially a matter of taking care of what takes care of you."

Whatever works. And you can't blame Gretzky for being somewhat superstitious, because there is no logical explanation for why he became the greatest player in the history of the sport.

When his teams have been tested for strength, Wayne has always been last. He bench-presses 140, which his mother could probably do. His skating speed, stamina, and peripheral vision are average, at best.

It used to be he would never work out in the offseason, although his advancing age, and his fitness-conscious wife, have changed that. He'll do just about anything for Janet. Almost.

"We had a $25,000 offer to have her shoot me out of a cannon," Gretzky said. "She wanted to do it, but I didn't."

Makes sense. Gretzky always has had a fear of flying.

I don't know if the superstars are flakey because they're superstars, or if they became superstars because they're flakey. I do know they are interesting people to deal with. Especially if you can get a couple of them together.

I had John Wooden and Bill Walton on the show together in 1992, and it was the first time they had sat down together on TV and talked about the amazing old days of the UCLA dynasty.

Bill, you'll remember, was the Bruins' resident hippie. Wooden wouldn't let Walton grow his hair long, but he didn't stop Walton from protesting the war, riding a bicycle in the Westwood traffic, or otherwise acting like a young man trying to express his convictions.

It was a classic culture clash—the conservative, Midwestern headmaster/coach and the Southern California beachboy/war-protestor. They clashed so badly that UCLA only won two national championships ('72 and '73) when they were together, and made the Final Four the other season.

The bonds—basketball and personal integrity—were stronger than the differences. And the mutual respect was profound even twenty years after the cheering.

In fact, the bond is stronger now, the passing of time having lent perspective to the amazing run of basketball that Wooden masterminded and Walton epitomized.

The day we were taping the show, Walton showed up very early at the studio. Wooden is a stickler for punctuality, and Walton was taking no chance of making the coach wait.

Wooden the coach was also a stickler for neat grooming among his players, and as Walton was in our makeup room being pow-dered, he panicked. He looked in the mirror and decided his hair was too long. He had Haley Cecile, our makeup artist, give him a quick trim.

Bill was wearing a coat and tie, of course, because Wooden always expected his boys to be neat and suitably attired for public functions.

Bill is outgoing, but usually in a low-key way, with a wry sense of humor. But that particular day he was very jovial and he was perspiring. What I'm trying to say is that he was nervous as hell. He was like a kid getting ready for his first date.

It's not that Walton and Wooden never see one another. They do often, they talk on the phone, they have kept close through the years.

But this was their first TV appearance together, and Walton didn't want to disappoint Coach.

When Wooden arrived at the studio I almost burst out laugh-ing. He was wearing a casual sweater and an open collar.

During one of the breaks Walton said, "Coach, did you ever think twenty years ago that someday we'd be on a talk show together and that you'd be wearing an open-collar shirt and I'd be wearing a jacket and tie? I even got my hair cut today."

Wooden smiled at Walton and said, "I noticed, William."

Wooden turned 82 in 1992, and he remains active. He exercises regularly, he serves as the unofficial godfather of college basketball, and he is a tireless and inspirational public speaker. He seems no less sharp than in his Wizard of Westwood days of the Sixties and Seventies.

Wooden did the first segment of the show with me, then Walton joined us for the second half of the program.

Bill, what was it about this man and his force that made great players even greater?

Walton: "Every day you woke up with great anticipation, knowing you were coming to the gym. I would always stop in his office before practice and say, 'Hey, Coach, what's goin' on? What are we doin'? How can I get more shots?'

"Every day it was so exciting, the intensity would just build throughout the day and finally at three thirty, when that whistle blew, everything had to be in perfect order—your water was already drunk, there were no drinks. There were no towels, there were no breaks.

"Two hours of nonstop basketball, at the highest level, with the greatest players and with the master sitting there, critiquing everything, never letting a single error go unnoticed or uncriticized, yet always pointing out the positive things, and building the team for the championship moment."

John, when you look back on the great teams, picking one is like picking favorite children, you can't do it. But can you pick out one or two remembrances of the Walton Era teams?

Wooden: "Well, of course we'll always remember the championship game (vs. Memphis State) in Seventy-three, where he made 21 out of 22 field goals. But now that picture (a photo) you're just showing, that back door. It worked perfectly with Bill because of his ability to pass. And his blocking shots. He's probably the best I've ever not just *had,* but *seen* on getting the ball out for the fast break. I've seen a lot of good rebounders that didn't get the ball out well."

Walton: "He mentions that game, he fails to mention that I was 2 for 5 from the line, with six turnovers."

We've got some photos of Bill Walton, the young activist. Here he is in Seventy-two, barricading the main building on campus, demanding a shutdown, sitting down on Wilshire Blvd., arrested for unlawful assembly, disturbing the peace. What did it do to the coach to see his star player doing these things?

Walton: "You didn't get those photos from my files, I know that. I think it disappointed John Wooden. I felt that he thought that I let him down, but he was understanding, he was understanding of my involvement as a student.

"And one thing that John Wooden did with each and every one of his players was allow them to be individuals. And we had many discussions about all of those things."

John, what did you learn from a young person's protests?

Wooden: "Well, I always felt that you have a right to protest, but in protesting, I don't believe you should deny others their rights. I felt the same way Bill did about the Vietnam situation, but I would go about it in a little different way."

Bill, is it true that you once asked Coach Wooden permission to smoke grass?

Walton: "No! We had discussions about all issues of the day, but I did *not* ask him that."

Somebody said there was a story that your knee was sore and you asked the Coach, "Do you think if I smoked marijuana, my knee would feel better?" For medicinal value only?

Walton: "No!"

But you always felt you could talk.

Walton: "When I left home in San Diego, I was very anxious to get away from home and get out from under parental supervision. I didn't realize I was getting under more supervision when I got to Westwood. But it worked out for the best, and the supervision that Coach Wooden had over all of his players took the place of our parents and really carried it on to the next level, and everybody came out the best for it."

In those days, the idea of a player smoking anything, or drinking, may have been cause for being thrown off the team. Then you bent a little bit, John, and you have said if you were coaching now, you'd say, ''Just don't tell me about it.''

Wooden: "Well, in my earlier years of coaching I had a number of rules and a few suggestions. In my later years of coaching I had fewer rules and more suggestions."

Walton: "The thing about Coach, though, the thing about John Wooden, was that the rules applied to everyone. The first practice of my senior year, after two straight national championships, two straight undefeated seasons, he threw me out of practice. He said, 'Bill, your hair's too long.' That's why I had to get it cut today."

We took a commercial break, and when we were off the air, Wooden said to Walton, "Bill, you know you did once ask me about smoking marijuana to help your sore knees."

"Did I?" asked Bill, his eyes wide.

"I would never forget a thing like that," Wooden said, smiling.

Michael Jordan, talking about his very first dunk, as a 5' 9" ninth grader:

"I remember I'd gotten a steal, I was on the break. I'd been trying to dunk in practice for so many times, and I never seemed to do it. I guess the intensity of fans, and the game, I went up to lay it in, not to dunk it, and I felt I was high enough to dunk the ball, and I kind of just flipped it over and dunked it. It was a baby dunk, but it was a dunk."

It was as historic a flight as the one the Wright Brothers made at Kitty Hawk. And sometimes I wonder if Jordan ever looks back and wonders if he did the right thing—wishes he had clanged that dunk attempt, said the hell with it and gone out for the golf team.

I admit it: I am fascinated with Michael Jordan. With what he does on the court, sure, but even more so with his life off the court. I am fascinated by his fate as a prisoner of fame.

Bob Greene, the Chicago *Tribune* columnist who wrote a book called *HangTime* on Jordan, compares him to Babe Ruth and Elvis. In terms of sports fame, Jordan certainly ranks, in recent years, with Magic Johnson and Muhammad Ali.

The critical difference is that Magic and Ali were like moths drawn to the spotlight. Jordan, off the court at least, is like a frightened deer caught in the headlights.

Even as he is making himself more famous and more recognizable each day in commercials and ads, he is growing more and more weary and wary of the fame.

I asked Jordan if he felt a prisoner.

"Yeah, a little bit," he said. "I kind of put this on myself. There's some advantages and disadvantages. Sometimes you want it. Initially, when I first got into the league, it was fun, I admit, to sign autographs and be recognized. But after a while it does get old, and now it's just something I have to deal with."

On the court he is the hunter. Off the court he is the prey, and it's always open season.

I was in Portland in the summer of 1992 during the pre-Olympic basketball tournament called the Tournament of the Americas. The U.S. Dream team was the attraction, of course, and Magic and Michael were the gods.

The worshipers amazed me. Every day, outside the hotel where the team was staying, thousands and thousands of fans would gather, and stand, and wait. For hours. All day. Just to catch a glimpse of Magic or Michael trotting onto a bus, or breezing through the lobby.

Even when the team bus would pull away and the people knew the Dream Team would not return for hours, hundreds would stay, as if reluctant to quit the vigil at this sacred shrine. At night, in the rain, they waited and waited.

I spent some time with Jordan that week and came away with very much the sense of Michael as prisoner. To do something impulsive, like stroll to a nearby park or catch a cab downtown to an ice cream store, was out of the question. Wherever Jordan went, his path was cleared by Secret Service types wearing suits and carrying walkie-talkies.

He even registered at two hotels, one under his real name and the other under an alias, to dilute the pressure.

He has tried disguises, wearing hats and sunglasses and such, but they don't work. Jordan is 6′ 7″, and besides, people recognize him by his body movement. You could put him inside an elephant costume and people would say, "My God, that elephant moves so gracefully, just like Michael Jordan."

I think Jordan wonders if he will ever have a life.

One of my first assignments as a TV rookie in Miami was to interview Don Shula, legendary coach of the Miami Dolphins.

That was good.

The interview was to take place at the Miami airport, where the Dolphins were returning after a heartbreaking, last-play loss to the dreaded Raiders in a playoff game.

That was bad.

I got to the airport with my crew at midnight, but the flight was delayed and didn't land until 3 A.M. As you might imagine, the delay only heightened the eager anticipation Shula had for meeting the press.

Shula is a man who takes himself extremely seriously. He can be funny, but get close to game time and you don't want to know him. And don't ever bother him with small talk and banter.

A no-frills, no-b.s. kind of guy. His favorite expression is, "Get the job done."

He got off the plane, started walking toward the terminal, saw me standing with my crew, camera lights on and microphone poised, and he said, "Awww, shit."

Instant rapport.

I tried to be tactful.

"Let me ask you a hypothetical question," I said. "What if you had been . . ."

He cut me off. "I don't answer hypothetical questions. Good night."

And he walked away. End of interview.

Another time, another interview with Shula: The occasion was Dolphins' assistant coach Bill Arnsparger leaving the team. Shula and Arnsparger were old and dear friends, Arnsparger was the architect of the Dolphin defense.

"Don," I said, "you know Bill so well, but you've never really talked about it from the standpoint of the love you have for him as a really good friend."

Shula made a face like he'd just stepped on a sharp tack.

"Give me a break," he said, and he got up and walked off.

Eventually we connected. I learned what to ask Shula, and when, and we had several great interviews. But there are no freebies with Shula—you get a good interview, you earn it.

Recently I was emcee for a fundraiser hosted by Shula, the charity being for breast cancer research and the foundation named after Don's late wife, Dorothy.

I was at the podium doing impressions and I noticed that Shula kept glancing over at his sons, Dave and Mike, and they would nod to him. Why? Because he didn't know any of the people I was impersonating and he wanted to know how I was doing. He had no idea how John Lennon sounded, or who the Bee Gees were.

When Don Johnson was filming *Miami Vice* in Miami, he wanted to visit a Dolphins practice. The team PR man, Eddie White, told Shula, "The *Miami Vice* people want to come over and watch a practice. Is that okay?"

"Sure," Shula said.

After the practice, White brought Johnson over to meet Shula.

"Don," White said to Shula, "I want you to meet another Don—Don Johnson, from *Miami Vice.*"

Shula shook Johnson's hand and said, "You guys are doing a wonderful job fighting crime in our city."

He thought Don Johnson was a real cop.

For Shula, the world outside of football did not exist. In one interview I asked him, "Tell me some people you admire."

He thought for a minute and said, "Tex Schramm is a guy I really admire."

A few questions later, still trying to draw him out, get him out of sports, I said, "Give me a man you admire who's completely out of football."

Shula said, "Well, Tex is out of football right now. Tex is a guy I admire."

Here's everything you need to know about Shula. When he met and fell in love with Dorothy and was considering asking for her hand in marriage, he took her to a field and asked her to backpedal—run backwards like a defensive back.

When I asked him about this story, Shula shrugged as if to say, "Doesn't every guy do that?"

He said, "I wanted to find out about her athletic ability. This was going to be a serious relationship and I wanted my kids to possibly be defensive backs, or if they were girls, to be cheerleaders. This girl was going to have to have a lot of coordination if I was going to continue to date her."

Of the great personal rivalries of sport—Russell vs. Chamberlain, Mays-Mantle-Snider, Martina vs. Chris Evert, Bird vs. Magic—the best ever just might be Jack vs. Arnie.

Arnold Palmer and Jack Nicklaus have battled almost weekly for the better part of three decades, and the battle still rages on, in a way.

In the golf world, these two are sort of like God and God Jr. Arnie invented the game and Jack perfected it. Arnie pried open the door of the vault and Jack walked in with a wheelbarrow. Arnie pioneered The Merchandising of the Athlete, and Jack carved out a massive corporate empire of his own.

But under it all, it's still about golf and about the two most intense competitors of the modern era of the sport.

Arnold Palmer took up serious golf at age five, plays it intensely every day still, and probably regrets those five years he wasted.

He broke one hundred at age seven, and will probably break seventy when he's one hundred.

His father was a golf pro and Arnie would tell his old man, "Watch, dad. Watch this."

"I suppose the guy I wanted to impress most was my father," Palmer said. "I spent most of my life trying to get his acknowledgment of what I was doing."

Arnie was a bit of a hell-raiser, but his life took a turn in 1950. He was attending Wake Forest. His best friend and golf teammate, named Bud, asked Palmer to ride with him to a dance at Duke. The two were inseparable, but Arnie was under the weather after having too much fun at a football game, so he declined. Bud crashed his car on the way to the dance and was killed.

Palmer's life instantly became more serious. He finished his semester and went into the service for three years. Then he went back to school, got a job, and won the U.S. Amateur Open.

Arnie was the ultimate hustler, the first of the really big athletes to market himself, the spiritual/economic forefather of Michael Jordan. In 1960 Palmer had contracts to endorse his own clothing line, shoes, shirts, golf cars, clubs, cigarettes, books, toys, and bug repellent.

He pioneered golf exhibitions and corporate golf outings. He was the first jock on the block to have his own jet airplane. He was a chain smoker and a chain new car–buyer.

He is still pretty much doing what he wants to do, which is play golf.

"I look forward to getting up every morning. I like to go to the office, do the things in the office, go back in the shop and work on some clubs, go have a light lunch at noon and then I'm out there playing."

Nicklaus once told me, "I don't love to be out there as much as Arnie does."

"Jack's told me the same thing," Palmer said. "I think certainly he has enjoyed the game. With the success he has had, there has to be a love in there somewhere for the game. But I don't think the less than important golf games are as important to him as they are to me."

Palmer was already the established superstar, the legend of golf, by the time Nicklaus came out of college and hit the tour.

"Of course, I watched Jack come along," Palmer said, "and my first reaction to Jack was to help him as much as I could. I remember when I first played with him, in an exhibition in Athens, Ohio, with Dow Finsterwald."

Palmer knew that Jack was going to be very successful. At that time, Palmer says he didn't anticipate that there would be a rivalry. Here was a young man who needed some help, and he says that he hopes he helped Jack.

Jack was always admired; Arnie was always loved. Do you understand why?

"No. Only way I can answer that, Roy, is to say that when I talk to you, I look at you. And when my fans are clapping, they're giving me the adulation they give me, I look at them, I look right in their eyes, and I think they like that."

I read Arnold a quote from Charlie Jones, an old friend of his.

"Loyalty's a two-way street with Arnold. If Arnold is playing in a golf tournament and you're there, believe me, you go out and you find out where he is and you stand by the gallery ropes. He sees everyone in the gallery and as soon as he goes by, he'll nod and motion or wave.

"If he doesn't see you there, the next night or the next time he sees you, he'll want to know where you were. 'I was playing and you weren't there.' He wants all his friends there."

Is that still true?

"I know who's there and who isn't. That's just one of my little idiosyncrasies, I suppose, that I notice. When my wife wasn't there, I looked and I knew; and my friends, same thing."

Palmer is proud of his competitiveness. He told me he doesn't see the same desire or work ethic on the tour today that he and Nicklaus brought to it. He feels the current players don't have the absolute compulsion to win of a Palmer or a Gary Player.

"I think age has taken a little of my fierceness away," Palmer said. "But there's nothing that can replace winning, and I still want to win, as much as ever."

As ultrafamous as Jack Nicklaus has become, as idolized as he is, I think he continues the elusive quest of Palmer in terms of sheer love from the fans.

No golfer tries harder than Nicklaus to accommodate the press, for instance, to reach out to the fans through the media, to be an ambassador.

I think he wants to be thought of as a good guy. When I asked Jack what there is about him that would surprise people to know, he said:

"My father was a great needler. I'm pretty much that way. I always love to be putting somebody on and kidding 'em and having fun with 'em. And I enjoy having them do it back to me. The serious mode that people see me in when I'm playing golf, they don't see the other side."

Greg Norman, we interviewed him and I'm sure he means no disrespect to you, but he said, "Jack has no life." That's a little strong, what I think he meant is you don't take as much time for yourself as you should.

"Greg's looking a lot at what I do right now. He didn't see me a lot when I was his age, when I spent an awful lot of time hunting, fishing, doing a variety of things. Now, my focus is a little different.

"My major focus is that I've got a business that I'm developing for my family. [Nicklaus's primary business is golf course design. At last count he had built eighty-two courses and had twenty-five more in the works.] We went through a sort of accounting analysis of my business about six years ago and they said, 'What would happen if you were gone? *You* are 90 percent of your business.' I said, 'That's not leaving a very good business to my family.' And so my whole thrust the last five years has been to try to develop a business that I can gradually drop out of, the (five) kids can gradually move into.

"So maybe I don't have a life from that standpoint, but that's the life I've chosen. Jackie (his oldest son) came to me not long ago and said, 'Dad, I've sort of stayed out of what you've done. I think it's time I picked up the responsibility. I want to take over where you are.' And I really look forward to that.

"My father passed away at age fifty-six, I'm fifty-one. And my father worked all his life to get in a position to semiretire so he could enjoy watching me play golf. He got some of it, but he never really saw the main part of my career, and I feel very, very bad about that."

I asked Nicklaus about the rivalry with Palmer for the affection of America's golf gallery.

What about the theory that the people never will completely embrace you like they embraced Arnie?

"Well, I don't have a problem. I probably wouldn't do that to me, either. I think that Arnold was the king, he's a very popular person, he's very much like a lot of people, he had his shirt out half the time, had a cigarette hanging out of his mouth and his hair was flying and he's hitching his pants, shrugging his shoulders, and he was Arnold.

"He related to the people, and rightly so. Arnold brought a lot of things into the game of golf that the golf game needed. He was a spark, it was a boost.

"And when you come along and you beat the king, people

aren't going to be happy. I didn't look much like an athlete at the time, I was big, burly, a little overweight, probably way too much overweight at the time. Baggy pants, hair shaved off. That was me. I never tried to be anyone else other than me, and that's all you can do."

People over the years have tried to get a feud going between you two, and I know you've said some very nice things about Palmer. In Golf Digest *you said, ''I never fought him, only his army.'' But you also said that there are things you don't like about Arnold and things he doesn't like about you.*

"I don't think there's any question about that. I imagine it would be the same with any two individuals you might pick. I think that Arnold leads a different life than I do. Arnold, the game of golf has always been his life, it's not been mine.

"I think for the most part, for two guys that have competed as heavily as we have throughout the years, I think we've been pretty darn good friends."

Is Palmer now a ceremonial golfer?

"When I won the Masters in Eighty-six, that was a phrase I used on myself. I said now I want to move into a ceremonial role. And I don't think Arnold's ever wanted to be a ceremonial golfer, he's always wanted to win.

"And frankly, I never could be a ceremonial golfer. I've tried, and I just can't go out and play and just be part of the scene. I've got to try to win, and I think Arnold's got to try to win."

Do you owe the game anything?

"I think we all owe the game. That's the only reason I'm playing any golf at all now, probably. I do enjoy playing golf, but I think the guys on the Senior PGA Tour, I think I owe it to them to play some golf.

"I think probably what's going to have to happen to me someday is when I'm not competitive anymore I'm going to have to quit playing."

TEN

TEACH YOUR CHILDREN WELL

My favorite guest on *Up Close* is my father, Bernard Firestone. He's on the show once each year, the Monday after Father's Day, and while some might consider this self-indulgent or corny on my part, his appearance is without question the most popular show every year.

Besides, it's my program and I love having Pop on with me. I consider him a great guest, very intelligent and interesting and theatrical. But I think the reason people like the Father's Day show so much is simply that it's about a father and a son. It touches something in almost everyone.

On the 1988 Father's Day show, Bernard and I talked a lot about boxing, one of many subjects on which he is very knowledgeable. He rhapsodized about fighters of the forties and fifties, great names from the past.

A couple of months later, I was in Atlantic City covering the Mike Tyson–Michael Spinks fight for ESPN. Tyson pulverized Spinks in the first round, and the media poured into the press interview area.

After Tyson did his TV interview in the ring, he was led into the main press interview room. Remember, only minutes before, he had been locked in the most emotional and warlike moment in sports, a heavyweight championship fight.

As Tyson walked into the room where about five hundred journalists on deadline were eagerly awaiting his comments, he spotted me, walked over and said, "Roy, can I tell you something? I saw the show with your dad and it was really great. I swear to God, I had no idea he knew so much about boxing! It was really impressive."

Tyson later told me his two favorite *Up Close* shows were that one with Bernard Firestone on boxing, and an appearance by boxer Bobby Czyz, who talked about how his father beat Bobby and the rest of the family for years, then committed suicide, a story we'll get into later in this chapter.

Without being overly psychoanalytical, I think Tyson picking those two shows is significant. He never really had a father and, in some ways, his problems in life have come from a lack of fatherly guidance when he really needed it. I think he is touched deeply by father-and-son stories, and I think just about everyone is.

With nearly every guest, especially those who are on more than once, we almost always wind up talking about their parents, and how those relationships affected their lives.

The most touching, frightening, enlightening, and passionate moments on the show have been set off by simple questions about a superstar's mom or dad.

I'm not David Viscott, I don't have profound conclusions to draw here about the cause and effect of it all. What seems pretty clear, though, is that fathers and mothers pass on enormous legacies, good and bad.

When Mike Garrett, the 1965 Heisman Trophy winner and former pro football star, was on the show, we played a film clip of his late father, a blue-collar laborer, talking about Mike.

"I get very emotional when I see this," Garrett said. "That's one of those nine-to-fiver guys the coaches in professional football talk about. They tell you, 'If you don't do well, you'll wind up a nine-to-fiver.' They didn't realize that when they threatened me with that, the nine-to-fiver guy was my hero. When they were doing that, they were making fun of my father."

Tears were rolling down Garrett's cheeks and he didn't bother to brush them away.

I don't think anyone ever expressed feelings for a father better than did Magic Johnson on the show a few years ago.

"My dad was my hero," Magic said. "He drove me, because I always wanted to be like him. My dad had two jobs, he had a truck and he hauled rubbish in the morning, from seven to about noon. Then he slept until two or three, ate, and went to work at the General Motors plant from four thirty in the afternoon until one thirty in the morning, came home, fell out again, and woke up at six.

"The one day I got to see him was Sunday. He said, 'If you want to spend time with me, you have to get up in the morning and go out with me, we'll talk. We'll talk about ball.' So I got up in the morning, went to work with him. He just instilled that hard work in me, and that's what I'm all about.

"I always asked him why he worked so hard. He said, 'Well, first of all, I have a family, and second of all, my father taught me to work.' He told me anything that I was gonna get, I was gonna have to work for. I said, 'But you don't have no time for yourself.'

"And he said to me, 'It's not all about that. I'm all about you, you and the other kids, makin' sure you're all clothed and so on. I'm all about you.' "

That phrase sticks with me: "I'm all about you."

I'm endlessly fascinated by the dad and mom stories of famous people. It's obvious that these superstar athletes are what they are, good or bad, in no small part because of their parents.

When I think of author Donald Hall's quote, that baseball is fathers and sons playing catch, I always think of Mickey Mantle. Mantle's father, Mutt, named his son after Mickey Cochrane, and he had a dream that the kid would become a great ballplayer and never have to work in the coal mines.

"From the time I was three or four years old," Mickey said on the show, "whenever I started running around, I had a ball, glove and bat in my hand. My dad became a miner, we moved to Commerce, Oklahoma, and he started working in the lead and zinc mines.

"He'd come home at about four or five o'clock. I know he had to be tired, but all he would do from the time he got home until dark was hit me pepper, fly balls, pitch to me. He'd pitch to me right-handed and my grandfather would pitch to me left-handed.

"I couldn't hit as good left-handed, but he told me, 'You got to keep on, someday you'll be as good a hitter left-handed as you are right-handed. And one of these days they're going to have platooning in baseball, right-handed hitters against left-handed pitchers.' The year I joined the Yankees, Casey [Stengel] started platooning, so my dad knew what he was talking about."

Mickey signed his first pro contract at eighteen, and a year later went to spring training with the New York Yankees.

"It was '51, and we went to spring training in Phoenix. I must have hit ten to twelve home runs, fifteen maybe. Anyway, it was an unbelievable spring, and that's when they started writing that I was going to be the next Babe Ruth, Lou Gehrig, and Joe DiMaggio all rolled up into one. Well it didn't happen. We got back to New York, I'm only nineteen years old and I think the biggest crowd I'd ever played for was like five hundred people at Joplin.

"I go to Yankee Stadium for the first time and there was 68,000 people. We're playing the Boston Red Sox. I started striking out quite a bit. I lost my confidence, I struck out five straight times in a doubleheader up at Boston and Casey took me out of the game, put somebody else in.

"We went from Boston to Detroit and Casey let everyone dress and go out on the field, then he sent the clubhouse guy to bring me back in. I knew I was gone. He sent me back to the minor leagues and he said, 'Just as soon as you get your confidence, we'll bring you right back.'

"I went to Kansas City and the first time up I bunted and got a hit. Well, George Selkirk was the manager and he called me over and said, 'Hey, Mickey, we know you can bunt, we want you to get in there and start hitting home runs, get your confidence back.'

"Well I didn't get another hit for twenty-two straight times. So I called my dad, got him out of the mines and said, 'Dad, this is Mick,' and he says, 'Yeah?' And I said, 'Well, I'm not doing too good.' He said, 'I've been watching.' I said, 'I don't think I can play ball.' He said, 'What?' And I said, 'I don't think I can make it.'

"He said, 'Where are you at?' and I told him I was at Kansas City. He said, 'I'll be right up there.' He drove all the way from Commerce up to Kansas City, and I'm thinking he's coming up to pat me on the back and say 'Hang in there' or something.

"He knocks on the door and I let him in. He just walks right past me and grabs my old suitcase and throws it down and he starts throwing stuff in it. 'What are you doin'?' 'Well,' he says, 'I'm taking you back home. You can work in the mines with me.'

"He said, 'I thought I raised a man, not a coward.' And he said, 'You're nothin' but a coward. You can just come back and work in the mines.' And of course he's got tears in his eyes, and it really tore me up to see him feeling that bad. So it took me about thirty minutes to talk him into letting me have another chance.

"But anyway, after he went home I started hitting and the rest is history."

I was working out at a health club one day in 1992, riding a stationary bicycle. A man riding the next bicycle turned to me and said, "I saw that show you did with Charles Barkley."

He was referring to a recent show on which Barkley had talked about his father, who left Charles and his mother when Charles was a year old.

On the show Barkley said, "I resented him when I was growing up because he wasn't there. And then it had always been on my mind, always. Then my uncle Sal passed away and I was kind of caught up [in whether or not to attempt a reconciliation with his father].

"I wanted to do it, but I didn't really know how to go about it because I wasn't really mature enough to go to my dad and say, like, 'Hey, Dad, I love you and I want to develop a relationship with you. 'Cause it's not easy. If you are away from someone ten, fifteen, twenty years, it's hard, because you don't know where to start.

"Our relationship right now is a lot better. One thing I want to say, if you are away from your mother or father, you need to do that [reconcile], because it's always going to be in the back of your heart, and I always missed my father, I always wanted to develop a relationship with him, but I didn't know how to go about it."

The all-time leading scorer, on the show to promote his latest book—*Wilt's Phone Numbers—The Early Years.*

A cherished moment: Ali surprises me on stage after my singing tribute to The Greatest.

Michael Burr

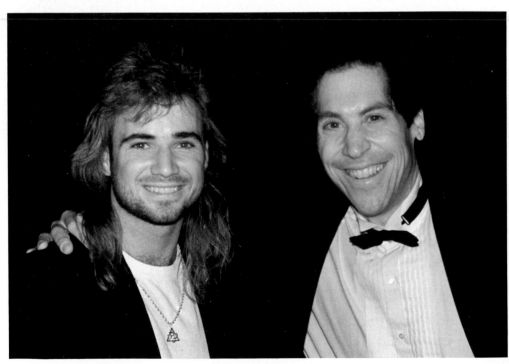

Here I'm giving Andre Agassi a special award for sitting through my nightclub act five times in one week. Get a life, pal.

Brian Janis/Phototechnik

Tense and solemn as always, Earvin Johnson struggles to express his feelings on life and basketball.

Getting the scoop from one of the good guys, Sugar Ray Leonard, at a big Las Vegas battle of the tuxedos.

"No, Roy, I don't think you could dunk if I loaned you my shoes and wristbands."

Stevie Wonder, explaining the game of basketfall from his truly unique perspective.

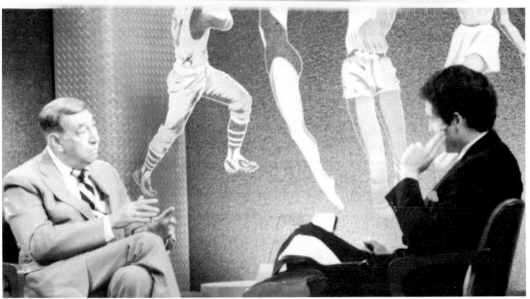

No, I am *not* asleep. It would be rude to sleep through a Howard Cosell journalism lecture. I am, however, mentally planning lunch.

"Okay, Mike, it's a deal. I'll teach you the left jab if you'll do my show Friday."

A fond reunion of two of the key figures in the Orioles' dynasty. Earl Weaver (right) was the fiery skipper. I was the only bat boy who could locate left-handed bats for Boog Powell.

Either Reggie is stunned that I'm getting a word in edgewise, or he's formulating a suggestion regarding the placement of my mike.

Obviously this man has forgotten that I threw a rock at his limo during the '68 Republican convention in Miami. Here, we reach an accord on Mookie Wilson.

Jon Soohoo

Anyway, back to the health club and the guy on the exercise bike: He said he liked the show with Charles Barkley, then he said, "I have a vested interest in that subject."

"Why?" I said.

"I'm Charles' father."

His name is Frank Barkley. We got into a nice conversation. I asked Frank if he would like to come on the show, and he said sure.

When he came on, I read a quote from a story in the Los Angeles *Times*, written by a man who grew up fatherless.

"The damage that is done to sons and daughters with absent fathers is staggering," the man wrote. "The emotional and psychological absence of a father renders a son lost in a veritable wasteland, mentorless, with no road map, he wanders throughout his life in search of his own selfhood. The current men's movement cannot make fathers pay for child support, but it can help some men look inside themselves, acknowledge their own wounds and attempt to be a real presence in the life of their kids."

I asked Frank Barkley why he had agreed to come on the show.

"I wanted to make sure that people really understand what leaving a child behind means," he said. "It's not where or why it happened, but there comes a time you have to make peace with yourself and the child. It's not so much that I was hurt the most, it's he who was hurt the most."

I mentioned that Charles had spoken of an anger he carries. I showed the film clip of Barkley elbowing the Angolan player in the Olympics and I asked Frank if he felt partially responsible for that anger.

"I am, I am, because I should've been there when he needed me, and when you're not there when a child needs you, the anger builds up in him. I promised him a lot of things, I promised to call him a lot of times, and he looked forward to these things, and when I didn't come through, he just got madder, so I can understand his feelings."

Frank described the reconciliation between him and Charles. It happened at the funeral of Frank's brother, who, on his deathbed, had made Charles promise to try to get back in touch with his father.

"We buried him on a Sunday morning," Frank said, "and it was the first time I'd ever seen my father cry. I was getting ready to leave, and Charles was waiting outside. He came in and said, 'Granddad, I'll see you when I come back.'

"So Charles was standing in the door and my daddy grabbed me and was crying and he said, 'Would you please take care of yourself? I'm gonna miss you.' And he was crying and shaking, and that's when I grew up, that's when I knew what a father was all about. I was forty-eight years old."

Frank and Charles were like strangers, but they both made the effort to develop a relationship. They started phoning one another, going to lunch, going to games.

I asked Frank what he lost in all those years of not knowing Charles or his other son.

"The love," he said. "To know I had someone to talk to, to be there with me on Father's Day. Those are lonely times, you know. Even though I work with kids, they aren't mine. He has a great mother, he has a great grandmother, okay? But there was a problem.

"One thing I got to say, Roy, is for a father to just be a father. It doesn't matter which way the wind blows, just take care of the kids."

There's something about prizefighters. Their relationships with their fathers and sons always seem pushed to the extreme ends of the scale, the beautiful and the ugly.

One of the most touching stories on the show was that of the late Max Baer and his son, Max Baer Jr., who played Jethro on *The Beverly Hillbillies.* Max Jr. came on the show and talked about his father.

Max Sr. was an amazing character, with huge amounts of charm and personality. He was heavyweight champion for a year, beating the hulking Primo Carnera in 1934 and losing a decision to James J. Braddock a year later. After losing to Braddock, Baer told the press, "I'm glad Jimmy won. He's got eight kids. I don't know how many I have."

Max Sr. never had the heart of a boxer, the anger or the killer instinct. He was a fun-loving, woman-loving man who got into boxing by accident. He got into a scuffle when he was seventeen, a man ripped his shirt and Max hit the guy and knocked him down.

Someone got him into a ring, he made $35 his first fight and figured he could retire on that. When the $35 ran out, Max kept going. One of his two wives said, "Max hated fighting. How he ever hit anybody I'll never know. He would never even hit his kids. He had no mean streaks. He was so very kind."

Max Jr. told about his father's death in 1958.

"He was at the Roosevelt Hotel in New York. He was shaving and he had a heart attack and fell to the floor. He crawled to the telephone and picked it up and he said, 'I think I'm having a heart attack, can you call me a doctor?'

"And the person said, 'Do you want me to call a house doctor?' and Dad said, 'Hell, no. I want you to call me a people doctor.'"

Max Jr. pulled out a letter he carried in his wallet, a letter his father wrote to him on his twenty-first birthday.

"I'll skip over the first part," Max Jr. said. "He says, 'I can't begin to tell you of the pitfalls that will be in your pathway along life's highway. Step around them, son, not into them. I'm not trying to frighten you, only to warn you so you'll never be heart-broken.

" 'I might not have been the father I could have been, but in my way I tried. Maybe I didn't know how to be. But if God were to say to me at any time, 'I must blind you, or take your life so that your dear ones can have health and happiness,' I kiss you all, if possible, and willingly go.

" 'You can't measure my love for you, Jim, Mom, and Augie. My son, may God always be in your corner, your future bring you much health, happiness, and success. Happy birthday, young man. I'm very proud of you and how you're thinking, doing, and acting.

" 'From a guy going down the other side of the mountain on life's highway. Dad.' "

One of our most unusual shows, and one of the saddest, featured two rival boxers who, instead of trading punches, traded child-abuse horror stories.

That was the show that Tyson had mentioned as being so moving to him, and with Tyson's own deeply troubled family history, I can see why.

I felt it was an important show, because every year in America, 2.5 million children are physically or sexually abused, and at least 1,200 of them die from the beatings. And that's just the reported and verified beatings and deaths, which may be only a third of the actual cases. Alcohol is a factor in about 80 percent of the cases. It is a horror, an epidemic that needs all the exposing it can get.

Bobby Czyz (pronounced Chezz) and Donnie Lalonde were on a promotional tour in 1992, drumming up interest in their cruiserweight title fight. Normally nothing remarkable comes out of these ticket-selling PR tours, but in this case, what we had were two intelligent, personable young men talking about growing up as brutalized victims of their fathers.

Czyz is a Jersey kid, and though he was raised in a middle-class family, he's a mean-streets kind of guy, like a character in a Martin Scorsese movie. He has an IQ of 140, was a straight-A student in high school, he recently ran for his area city council and won. Very impressive vocabulary.

His mom, Louise, doted on Bobby. His father, Robert Sr., loved Bobby almost to death. He routinely beat and bullied everyone in the family, especially Bobby and Louise.

It would take several psychiatrists to sift through all the emotional rubble. But here's the story in a nutshell: Robert Sr. lost *his* father when he was two, and he was beaten regularly by a day-care center employee. His mother died after a car wreck, with Robert having to pull the plug on her life-support system. He was extraordinarily intelligent, compulsively neat and well-dressed, physically imposing, and systematically, sadistically abusive.

"He felt he was cheated somehow," Bobby said, "and certainly he was cheated out of a dad."

Robert Sr. and Louise had three sons and a daughter. Bobby was the oldest, and Robert Sr. loved that kid.

"He told me on a regular basis, from the earliest I can remember, that I was the greatest man on the planet," Bobby said.

But the anger and pain Robert Sr. carried inside him oozed out like poison from an open sore. He was a frustrated boxer and a brown belt in karate. He beat Louise for tiny oversights. To this day, her jaw aches when it rains.

One day Bobby broke an ankle in a pickup basketball game, which knocked him out of an upcoming boxing competition. His father came home, saw the cast, "Walked over and punched me dead in the mouth. He said, 'I owe you that.'

"What it was, it hurt him so bad that I had hurt myself, it tore his heart out because it was his dream that I be a fighter. He only had violence and trauma in his life, and that's what he dealt through. Beatings got results when he was a kid, so even though he was an adult and could reason, he knew it got results.

"At one point I told him, 'Dad, we love you, but we don't like you, you're mean.' He said, 'I'll try,' and for two weeks he was gold, he was a normal dad, it was great, things were going good. But I sensed a real strain, I sensed that he was working at this. Not only was it not coming natural, but he wasn't enjoying it. After two weeks he told me, 'Listen, I don't like being nice. It makes me ill. You accept me for what I am, 100 percent, or not at all.' I said, 'Fine, then accept me the same way.'

"I went to him for my eighteenth birthday, I said, 'I'm a man now, this is what I want for my birthday: Don't ever hit my mother again.' He looked me straight in the eye and said, 'I cannot do that, I cannot give you that promise. Just know that, as often as I hit her, it would've been more if you hadn't asked.' I can't reconcile that, I can't do it."

Why didn't Bobby leave home or go to the police?

"You could not get a restraining order that would shorten his arms or his reach. You could run away but you could not hide. If anything happened in that house that was out of his control, my mother, who is stronger than I'll ever be, would pay for it, she would die, and that handcuffed me to the house."

Finally Bobby's youngest brother couldn't take the abuse. He was talking about moving out of the house, out of what Bobby calls "a mental straitjacket." The middle brother sided with the youngest brother, and Bobby sided with both of them. Robert Sr. ordered the two younger brothers to move out of the house. It was the summer of 1983.

"He freaked out on me a little bit and told me he was throwin' me out, too. And he got a little carried away, he always said things he didn't mean, but he said something to the effect, 'You could go off with 'em, and leave your money here. It's mine. I made you, and without me, you're nothing.' But I was raised to be a man and I had a few things to say about that. I said some things I didn't mean and the last thing I said to him was, 'I tell you what, I got two brothers now, and I got no father.'

"I went out to walk the dog. We had a little dog that we'd found and my little sister became attached to it so we kept it. I came back and he never even acknowledged my existence. I tried to apologize, I stood between him and the TV, he had this easy chair he used to lay in. I could not get an apology across. Twenty minutes I tried to talk to him, I mean, the man didn't even blink. I wasn't there. He didn't curse at me or tell me off or yell, not a word.

"I went to bed. Finally I came down, he was slumped over a chair, he'd shot himself."

As terrible as Bobby's father had been, he had also loved and encouraged Bobby in his career. He even called his son Chappie because that's what Joe Louis called his trainer, Jack Blackburn. Bobby had CHAPPIE stitched on his boxing robe.

To this day, Bobby's father visits him in a recurring nightmare.

"He knocks on the door, I open the door and there he is, he has a hole in his head, which I can't ever get out of my mind, because when I found him, that's the way he was. He's bleeding and he has his suit on, and his coat over his arm, and his briefcase, and he hands it to me and says, 'Give this to your mother, tell her to put dinner on now, I'll be down in five minutes.' And he walks upstairs to take a shower, which was what he always did."

In the nightmare, Bobby shouts after him, "Dad, you've been dead eight years! You killed yourself!"

The thing is, Bobby still loves his father. He thinks Robert Sr. felt himself growing more violent and blew himself away in an ultimate gesture of love.

"My father was great, there's no question about it. He's the reason I got straight A's in school, the reason I'm a good fighter, the reason I'm successful. He instilled the right things in me. He may have implemented them with the wrong manner, but it was for the right reasons. When I was a kid, no one could ever say a bad word about him, that would constitute a fist fight on the spot. I'm very proud of him. I carry his name."

Lalonde also had a chilling tale of abuse.

"I remember times walking in the door two minutes late and being knocked out by my stepfather. By punches. Out cold, many times. And he would turn on the heat elements of the stove and put my brother's face right up to it and try to push it right in there. Horrible, physical beatings

"Every time my parents would go out and drink, we would be literally under the beds, scared to death about what was gonna happen when they come home, because they'd be fighting and, in turn, would turn to the kids.

"I left home at fifteen, got myself together as a person, which took a lot of years. Then I just phoned him one day and said, 'I'd like to get together for lunch.' I hadn't seen him in twelve years. I said to him, 'I just want you to tell me what I as a child did to you to make you want to do that to me.' He just broke down completely and let it all out, about what he put us through."

Lalonde and Czyz are both crusaders against child abuse. Lalonde visits hospitals and he told me of seeing one boy with BAD KID burned onto his chest with the tip of a cigarette. I asked if those sights bring back bad memories.

"Not so much memories as feelings," he said. "Yeah, it just twists like a rope that's all knotted and turned real hard inside your heart."

Boxing is a fascinating sport to me, but when these two guys are involved, it takes on a different and scary meaning. You would think they had experienced enough violence.

At one point Lalonde did get out of boxing because he couldn't reconcile the violent profession to his peaceful crusade against child abuse. He came back to the ring, in part, to give himself a stronger forum from which to express his views.

"I don't consider boxing violence," he told me. "I consider it an art that I'm trying to perfect."

Czyz, as a boxer, doesn't try to bury the past.

"One thing I obtained from my childhood, that Donnie didn't, is a vicious streak, a mean streak, real mean, to the bone. Outside the ring, I'm the nicest guy in the world, but my father prepared me to be vicious. He was vicious, and he believed that it was a man's place to have a vicious side to protect his family. I've just taken that and redirected it and focused it in the ring."

When they fought a week later, Czyz opened several cuts around Lalonde's eyes, bloodied his nose, knocked him nearly out of the ring and defended his title with a unanimous decision.

Ready for a more uplifting story? Wes Unseld, the coach of the Washington Bullets, told how his parents' love has shaped his entire life. He was one of nine children, yet this is how close he was to his father, Big Charles: Wes was on a road trip when he decided he wanted to marry his sweetheart, Connie. Wes phoned Big Charles, who went to Connie's house, got down on his knees and proposed marriage on behalf of his son.

Big Charles was a bricklayer, a huge man. He died of a heart attack.

"I have no doubt that he worked himself to death for his kids," Wes said. "My mother worked and sacrificed, too. I remember one time overhearing my parents argue, my father trying to get my mother to buy a dress. She was saying somebody in the family needed shoes, and I remember him saying, 'You haven't had a dress in years.' Things like that stick with you."

Then Wes made one of the most eloquent statements about family that I've ever heard.

"To me," he said, "the best thing my father did for all nine of his kids was very simple. He loved our mother. That kept us all together, and right now we are all as close as can be. I'm basically what my parents made me."

There seems to be no consistent formula to successful parenting, no secret. Except love. That's the one thread running through all these stories, the strong correlation between parental love and a loving child.

Two great parents is the ideal situation, but one strong parent, it seems, can do the trick. Karl Malone, for instance, despite his ferocity on the court, is as nice and honest and simple a person as you would want to meet.

His father passed away when Karl was very little, and his mother raised nine children with hard, hard work, love, and almost no money. They lived in tiny Summerfield, Louisiana, population 250, as rural as you can get.

How country is Karl? Here he is, giving his Michelin guide to squirrel stew:

"The cat squirrel is great, they're more tender. And the fox squirrel, which is sort of brown-reddish, they're more tougher, they're more of a pine-tree squirrel. You take 'em and you skin 'em, get all the hair off 'em, then you put 'em in a stew.

"My brothers used to go huntin' and we'd have the squirrels for breakfast. Homemade biscuits with squirrels. They'd shoot 'em with shotguns and you'd bite into some of the shots."

The center of Karl's universe was, and still is, his mother. He has a wife and two children now, but he still phones Mom at least once a day.

"I know a lot of people can say, 'Hey, my mom is the greatest,'" "Mailman" said. "When I say it, I always get a lump in my throat, because my mom raised nine kids by herself, and we never went a day in our life without food. My mom would do without things, no shoes. She worked in a sawmill. She would put cardboard from boxes in the bottoms of her shoes. And you know how long it takes for cardboard to get wet.

"She would do things like that so she could buy us shoes and clothes. It was to the point where we never wanted food, but we didn't have bicycles, things like that. She would say, 'Just hang in there, God will bless us.' Things finally did start happening for us, but it took a long time. It makes you really appreciate it when you do get it. You don't take it for granted.

"When I went to college at Louisiana Tech, Mom said, 'Do one thing. Have people love to see you comin'. Always. Don't have 'em mash your fingers gettin' you out the door. Have them want you to stay.'"

If baseball is fathers and sons playing catch, here is basketball: When Karl first showed an interest in the game, his mother would help him practice. She would hold her arms out in front of her, forming a hoop, and Karl would shoot paper wads or rolled-up socks through the hoop.

"My mom worked two or three jobs, and that was her way of

spendin' time with her son. What I've learned, Roy, is if you look at a lot of successful people, they tend to appreciate things more when they had to work to get it. That's how I was.

"And that's how it is in society, I think we do too much on the big material things. My ideal day is wakin' up, havin' breakfast with my family, goin' out, startin' my tractor and headin' off to the field to cut hay. And on an off-day, going' fishin', goin' huntin'. It's a simple life and I know some people might laugh, but I wouldn't trade that for anything in the world.

"It never was a dream of mine to play professional basketball. It's still not a dream. So therefore I don't let things like this go to my head."

It seems like a lot of the very successful coaches were raised under hard conditions financially. Joe Paterno, possibly the most decent and honorable football coach in the land, talked about his mother and father giving up movies, scraping together twenty bucks a month to send Joe to a Jesuit school.

Dale Brown, the spacey but successful LSU basketball coach, grew up with nothing. His father ran out on his mother when Dale was three, left them penniless.

"I like challenges," Dale said, "I guess because I was the small guy that wasn't supposed to make it. My wife and daughter have told me, 'Please don't tell that story, it sounds like you're looking for sympathy.' I'm not, the only reason I tell this story is that there are a lot of down-and-outers watching this program, who probably think you have to be born with a silver spoon in your mouth to succeed. I wasn't, I came from poverty.

"My mother was one of the two most pathologically honest people I've ever met, I would say she is probably a saint. One of the things that's burned into my mind was one day when I came home for soup. We couldn't eat at the school because we didn't have any money. I came home and a welfare worker was there. She said, 'Mrs. Brown, Ward County Welfare can no longer afford you. You're getting $42.50 a month from us.'

"The welfare woman pointed to me like I was a dog and said, 'Can't he get a job?' Well, I was working, I had a paper route and I'd pick up Coke bottles from ditches.

"I saw the same thing happen with the landlady, intimidating my mother and making her cry, and I remember that day saying, 'Never again will I ever be silent and see an injustice done, and I think that was the catalyst for me being committed to what I do."

The effect of a father on his son can be as strong as the moon on the tides. Two men whose athletic destinies were directly shaped by their fathers are James Toney and Pete Maravich. Toney is the product of a nightmare; Maravich of a dream.

Toney is the International Boxing Federation world middle-weight champion. His mother, Sherry, had him when she was seventeen. He was raised mainly by his grandmother. James's father left Sherry when James was small, but not before abusing her to a remarkable degree. For example, he shot her in the leg.

When Toney was on the show, we flashed a quote of his from a story in *Sports Illustrated* regarding his father: "Everything is about that, the feeling of the abuse. I look at my opponent and I see my dad. So I have to take him out, I have to kill him. I'll do anything I have to do to get him out of there."

I asked James if he stood by that statement.

"Definitely, everything I said in that article I meant. It's the pain he put my mom through, and myself. Here I'm twenty-three years old, growing up all these years without a father, he abandoned us when I was young, my mother had to struggle through the early years with him."

I mentioned the situation with Charles Barkley, how Barkley seems to have found some peace of mind through reconciliation with his father, or at least some understanding. Toney wanted no part of that kind of talk.

"Barkley's father didn't shoot his mother in the leg and slam her leg in the car door."

The anger Toney carried around was aimlessly directed for many years. He was constantly in trouble in school and on the streets, dealing crack at one point, even though he didn't really need the money. Then he learned to focus that anger in the socially accepted form of violence called boxing.

I asked Toney a hypothetical question: If he could somehow rid himself of the hate for his father, clean it out of his system, would he want to do that? And he said no. Without that violent anger, he would be just another kid in the neighborhood. With it, he is a world champion.

By the way, you can draw your own conclusions about boxers and tormented childhoods. I will say this: If you had a decent, reasonably nonviolent and nontraumatic upbringing, you can probably kiss that ring career goodbye.

Pete Maravich is, in some ways, the most fascinating character in recent sports history. His father, Press, was a great player himself, but his career was cut short by military service, before he went on to become a famous coach at LSU.

Press had a dream: To revolutionize basketball.

To understand what Press wanted to do, picture that shoe commercial, where Scottie Pippen goes into basketball's past and plays against a bunch of slow, methodical white guys who are absolutely dazzled by this incredibly gifted and creative player.

Press was a product of that old-time basketball, but he envisioned a game that was wide open and beautiful and fast and endlessly creative. To bring that game to life, he needed a person to grasp the dream and put it out on the basketball floor.

Along came Pete. Press invented a million basketball drills and Pete practiced a million and one. Eight hours or more every day, year after year. Press would drive his car and Pete would lean out the window, dribbling. Pete would sit on the aisle at the local theater, dribbling through the entire movie.

He became Pistol Pete, the highest scoring player in college history, and then a great pro who was burdened with bad teams and bad knees. In pro basketball history, Pete rates only a colorful footnote for his statistical achievements. But there's no doubt he helped change the game of basketball, styelwise, as much as guys like Dr. J and Magic.

It was an amazing father-son blend. Press had the dream, and Pete, instead of rejecting the dream because it was shoved down his throat, took it into his own heart and soul, almost as if it had been surgically transplanted.

Pete came on the show in 1987. He was long since retired from basketball, and had become a born-again Christian. I read Pete a quote from David Halberstam: "Press consciously or unconsciously gloried in Pete's achievements and his reflected fame. Father and son, with identities too close for the good of either."

I asked Pete if he agreed with Halberstam's assessment.

"Not really," he said. "My dad always had a dream, to make basketball something that was not as stagnant and fundamental, he wanted to elevate it, he wanted to kind of revolutionize it himself. He was a heck of a basketball player, but because of the war he couldn't do what he wanted to do.

"He really handed that dream down to me, he wanted me to fulfill that dream, and really, that's what I did, Roy, for him."

Pete was a very, very intense man, he looked you square in the eye and spoke straight from the heart. I asked him how devastating it had been to lose his father, and Pete said:

"It was very devastating, but in fact I really don't have any pain, because I was there for his last breath. I was with him for five straight months, twenty-four hours a day. I traveled some twenty thousand miles trying to get treatment (for kidney disease) for him. I carried him places, like he used to carry me in the backseat of the car to camps in the summer.

"We were very, very, very close, and I think that's good, I think a father and son should be that close, I think our heroes today should be the fathers, should not be the athletes. You can admire athletes, you can admire rock stars, but it should be the fathers that are the heroes of kids. Most kids like to be like their fathers, the ones that show them love."

Pete talked about his son, Jason, who was eight at the time. Pete tried to coach Jason in basketball but as sons will sometimes do, Jason rejected the coaching, said he didn't want to be a basketball player.

The NBA Entertainment people happened to send Pete a tape of an NBA All-Star program. Pete gave the tape to Jason, who tossed it in a pile. Not interested.

"Within two months," Pete told me, with a little pride and a lot of amazement, "he had watched that tape some seventy-five times, he knew every player, every move, and it got him out and playing."

A month after Pete was on the show, he was playing pickup basketball and he dropped dead of a heart attack at age forty. But the dream lives on, on every basketball court.

Athletes pick up labels, and the label on Bobby Bonds, a dangerous hitter for fourteen seasons in the Seventies and Eighties, was that he never fully achieved his potential, partially due to drinking problems.

But his son, Barry, is one of the truly great young players in the game, and he says that Bobby lived up to every ounce of his potential as a father.

"My father was something special to us," Barry said. "He was our best friend, and your best friends in life make mistakes, but we love him no matter what.

"He was always a big inspiration for me. He was there for me. When things went bad, I could pick up a telephone and I could call him, that helped a lot."

They are different. Barry is an outgoing, extremely personable and delightful guy. Bobby is less outgoing.

"We call him the one-word man," Barry said, "because trying to get him to evaluate something, you can forget it. He says, 'Can you see it [the baseball]?' 'Yeah.' 'Then hit it.'

"Those are my dad's answers. In Bobby Bo's [Bonilla's] situation, he scrunched down [in the batter's box] one time, in San Francisco, and my dad's talking with him, he says, 'Bobby Bo, are you comfortable?' He said, 'Yeah.' My dad said, 'Well hit that way.' That's my dad. Bobby Bo went out and hit an upper-deck home run."

I had Barry and Bobby on the show together once, and the love they share is evident.

"Barry and I, with my other two kids, have always been extremely close," Bobby said. "It's always been friend, buddy, then father. I've always told him, I can be your friend, buddy, or your father. The buddy system seems to work the best.

"When they were little, they came to the ballpark with me, I played baseball with them, worked out with them, I would go to their Little League games. I used to sit up in my car and look through the trees, so they wouldn't know I was there, because I felt that would put pressure on them.

"I had the Wiffle balls and Nerf balls and was pitching to them, I did all the things that fathers do.

"He has a lot of me in him, because of the determination and what he wants to achieve, which makes me as proud as any man in the country. I won't ever forget the first game I went to watch him in Pittsburgh. I had to go hide, because he hit a home run and I jumped up and down and I caught myself, because I really don't try to get that emotional. I really felt embarrassed for him, that his teammates were going to say, 'Look at Barry's father, acting like a nut.'

"But I was more overjoyed probably than he was, to see my son achieve, and to know what he's gone through, the struggle and the battle.

"So when I watch him play I'm just totally elated. It's just a tremendous feeling."

My father never played catch with me.

Bernard was not athletic. He didn't teach me how to throw a football, it wasn't a Field of Dreams father-son relationship.

What he taught me, among other things, was a love for sports. He has a great knowledge of sports and a great sense of theatrics and of what is significant and dramatic in the games.

I would sit with him and listen to or watch games, and ask questions. "What does 'three-and-two' mean?" "Why are there so many guys named Alou in baseball?"

He would tell me why things were significant, the meaning of Jackie Robinson, the feeling of going to a Giants game at the Polo Grounds. He told me who wore the white hats in sports, who were the bad guys. He told me all about this amazing Babe Ruth character.

Pop has always been an enormous supporter of my career. My senior year in college, I got a job as an intern at the CBS affiliate in Miami—eighty bucks a week, fifteen hours a day, mostly scraping glue off a hot-splice editor. Occasionally I got to go out with a crew as a cameraman.

My dad wanted to help me advance. He was a member of a health club where Bernie Rosen, the station manager, also worked out. One day Dad approached Rosen in the locker room and asked him if I was ever going to get a chance to do any voice-overs or on-camera stuff.

Rosen told Pop, "Roy's the worst cameraman I've ever seen. When he goes on assignment, it's even money he'll leave the equipment behind on the field."

True. I left an expensive camera on the roof of a car, drove off and bounced the camera along a freeway. But my dad persisted with Rosen. "Is he going to be an intern all his life?"

I don't know what effect that had, but eventually they let me do some on-camera work, and within a year of graduating from college, I was the sports anchor at the rival ABC-TV affiliate, WPLG. My dad was unbelievably proud.

And now I'm unbelievably proud when Bernard Firestone comes on the show once a year.

He's never had training in journalism or TV, but he still has that great ability to paint word pictures, to bring a poetic touch to the games.

He talks about watching DiMaggio, Bobby Thomson, Dusty Rhodes, Willie Mays. In the Navy he got to be friends with Stan Musial, Johnny Pesky, Billy Herman. Bernard is an expert on the great fighters of the Forties and beyond, and he can discourse eloquently on the evolution of the social consciousness of sport.

If you think I'm a ham, tune in next Father's Day and see where I got it. Dad is so comfortable on the show, at times he'll even break into song.

When he was on in 1991, Pop forgot to say, "I love you" at the close of the show. It bothered him all year. So in 1992, he closed the show with, "And this time, I love you."

I said, "Thanks, I love you, too."

ELEVEN

REBELS WITH
AND WITHOUT
A CAUSE

People ask me, "Is Reggie Jackson an egomaniacal jerk, or is he a brilliantly fascinating and charming guy?"

My answer is yes.

Reggie and I go way back together. At least I think we do. Maybe I'm imagining the whole thing. I am sure that he never has been a guest on my TV show, having turned down invitations. However, once when I was on vacation and I turned on my hotel room TV, there was Reggie Jackson, guest-hosting *Up Close*.

I would like to stress that I always was a big fan of Reggie the ballplayer. When Reggie Jax was coming to bat, I never went out for a hot dog, even though you would think the sight of Reggie coming to bat would make you hungry for a hot dog. He was elected to baseball's Hall of Fame, overwhelmingly, in January 1993 and I enthusiastically endorsed the vote.

He was electrifying. One of the most dramatic swings of all time. Truly an exciting and theatrical ballplayer. I loved watching him play with the Oakland A's, then the Baltimore Orioles.

Then he became a Yankee, and I met him, and . . . well, let's flash back to that fateful day in the spring of 1977. I was a rookie sports reporter for Miami TV station WPLG. It was the opening day of spring training, and I was at the Yankees' ballpark in Ft. Lauderdale with my camera crew.

It was the first day Reggie ever wore the historic pinstripes. I wanted to interview him, but I approached him warily, because he had a reputation for being very, very tough on reporters. Would he do an interview?

"Sure! You bet! Glad to, Roy."

Before or since, I don't think I've ever talked to a more accessible, open, reflective, introspective, quotable guy than Jackson was that afternoon. He talked about his father, Martinez, how Reggie admired him above everyone in his life. He talked about what it is to wear the Yankee pinstripes, to carry the torch of black Yankee players passed down through the years, starting with the great Elston Howard.

And on and on. I was thinking, man, I don't know how the hell this guy got a rep for being tough to interview. They've got him pegged wrong. Forget about just athletes, this is one of the greatest *people* I've ever met in my life. Terrific guy.

I'm twenty-one years old, just out of college, a nobody, and he's calling me Roy, looking me in the eye like we're old pals.

One of the projects I was working on for the station was a short, fun-type feature on ballplayers and money. I was going to get comments about money from several players and edit them together and put them to music.

Reggie was making $450,000 a year, a monstrous sum at the time. I asked him if we could talk about money.

"Money, Roy, is nice, but more than anything it's a point of pride, because it took me a long time to get where I'm at financially, it took me a long time, six full years, before I made a hundred thousand."

Later that day I talked with several other Yankees—Catfish Hunter, Roy White, Billy Martin. Then I went back and edited the "Money Machine" story. I took quick cuts from several interviews and overdubbed the James Taylor song "Money."

I used Reggie's bite about taking six years to make it to $100,000. It wasn't a Pulitzer Prize piece, but it was a cute feature for that night's news.

The next day I went back to Yankee camp. Apparently Reggie

saw the piece and didn't enjoy it. He felt I had interviewed him under false pretenses, conned him, although at that stage of my career I couldn't have conned a kindergartner. When I walked into the clubhouse, Reggie greeted me with something like this:

"You ——, you ——, I oughta break you in half. Who do you think you are, ——? I give you my time and then you hammer me?"

Several of the players were watching, and Reggie pointed to me and warned them, "Don't talk to this ——!"

I felt extremely bad. I'm a kid, a Reggie Jackson fan, and he hates me.

Well, I still had a job to do, so I was back the next day—same ballpark, same team, same Reggie. Or was it? I was standing near the batting cage. Reggie sauntered over, unsmiling, stuck out his hand and said, "Reggie Jackson."

I said, "Hi, Reggie. Roy Firestone."

"Roy, nice to see you. Can I help you with anything?"

Was he burying the hatchet? Setting me up? Putting me on? Getting ready to break me in half? I have no idea.

Now we fast-forward to 1981, the World Series, Yankees vs. Dodgers. I had moved on to Los Angeles, to KNXT, and I was covering the Series. In a game at Dodger Stadium, Reggie misplayed a fly ball and the Dodgers won. Me and about five hundred other print and electronic reporters were working the postgame clubhouse. I approached Jackson's locker, mike in hand, camera and lights on, and quietly asked him if he would explain what happened on the fly ball.

"You turn that —— light out of my face or I'll slam it down your —— throat," he explained. "Get the —— out of here. Who the —— do you think you are?"

I figured it was the lights, so I had the cameraman shut them off, but Reggie continued.

"You come in here askin' me like I'm a —— lunatic, like I'm gonna answer your question when all you're trying to do is make me look bad."

I said, "I'm not trying to make you look bad, all I'm trying to do is . . ."

"Yes you are. You could see that I was out there like a ——

drunk trying to catch the —— ball, I did my best, if I'd'a caught it, it would've been one of the greatest —— catches of all time. Now get the —— out of here, ——, and don't ever talk to me again."

I went back to the newsroom and edited Reggie's speech, bleeping out the bleeps, and played it back on the news that night.

I wasn't exactly a veteran in the business yet, but by then I'd been around enough to know a little more about Reggie, to know that I wasn't the first reporter he had bullied. I didn't want to launch a campaign on behalf of a beleaguered press, but I don't think it's honest if the media portrays athletes only in the most favorable light. It was an honest slice of baseball life, and an honest glimpse of Reggie's personality.

The bit got a lot of attention. John Hall of the Los Angeles *Times* mentioned it in his column, and L.A.'s leading radio sports personality, Jim Healy, gave the audio of the "interview" prominent play.

I saw Reggie the next day at the ballpark and he wanted to kill me, and probably refrained only because it would look bad on his resumé. He started to yell at me and I said, "Look at it this way, Reggie. You treated me like dirt, and you don't even know me."

He said, "I know you! I know you from Miami. You're the hammer guy, the guy who hammered me."

And I'd always thought the hammer guy was Hank Aaron.

Then Reggie looked at me, stuck out his right hand and said, "Friends?"

In the offseason he signed with the Angels, and I went to their spring training ballpark in Palm Springs. I was standing in the dugout when I felt a tap on my shoulder.

There was Reggie, right hand extended.

"Roy Firestone?"

"Yeah."

"Reggie Jackson. We gonna start off on the right foot?"

"We've never been on the wrong foot, Reggie."

"Let's have a great year, then. We've always been close."

What do I think of Reggie Jackson? Well, one phrase he coined is "The magnitude of me." At the moment he realizes you have value to him, in terms of maximization of his media image, reflecting the magnitude of Reggie to the public in the best light, you are his pal, you are his minister of propaganda.

If there's not much you can do for him, he'll return the favor and not do much for you.

Typical scene with Reggie: I'm at the ballpark before a game. I've got to do a five-minute stand-up interview, live, at 5:30. I ask Reggie, "Can we get you for the five thirty live spot?"

"Sure, babe. I'll be there. What time is it now? We got ten minutes, I'll be there. Just got to finish my hittin'."

Now it's 5:29 and counting, I'm waiting by the dugout, here comes Reggie.

Ah, but Reggie does a U-turn, calling out over his shoulder, "Oh man, I forgot my sunflower seeds."

Or, "Hey, I gotta hit, man. I'm workin' now, this is my office. If I can accommodate you, I will, but my work comes first."

But you promised, Reggie.

After a couple of these live interviews with no one live to interview, I stopped asking Jackson. A guy with Reggie's magnitude leaves a big void when he stiffs you for that live TV stand-up.

I've seen Reggie give the best interviews in sports. I've also seen him humiliate and harass and threaten reporters with great harm.

I've seen him sign autographs in the hot sun, chatting it up with little kids (usually when there's a camera rolling). I've also seen him curse and berate little kids who bother him for autographs.

I've seen him offer money to former teammates down on their luck. I understand he gave one former teammate a blank check. There's a story that when he played in New York, he came upon an accident victim lying in the street, and comforted the person until the ambulance arrived, telling him, "It's okay, man, this is Reggie."

He could be incredibly sincere and endearing, to the point he would even have me thinking, "Maybe it's *me.* Maybe *I'm* nuts. Maybe he's right, *I'm* the ——head."

Then I would see him go the other way. Lecture and curse a frail old clubhouse security cop because an autograph seeker got to Reggie. Present himself, naked, to a female reporter in the clubhouse and say, "What do you think of this?"

And it wasn't just the press and fringe people he would annoy. When the A's traded Jose Canseco in 1992, A's manager Tony LaRussa defended the trade by talking about how Jose's bad attitude carried over onto the field.

LaRussa, who played with Jackson in Oakland, said, "With superstars, there are certain things you have to put up with. Like Reggie Jackson, for instance. Reggie could really be an ass——, but when it came time to play, he was there, so his teammates could put up with him being an ass——."

Yet, as I've said before, I don't pick guests for my show based on my own personal likes and dislikes. So Reggie has been invited several times. Always said no.

Once he said yes. A couple years ago he was promoting some product and I invited him to be a guest. I figured we could work out our differences on the air, have a little encounter session, talk about our problems with one another. It might be interesting.

"Sure, we'll do it, Roy," Reggie said.

Then, at the last possible moment, I got a call from Reggie's representative. "He says he can't do it, that you're a hammer guy, you're trying to hammer him."

And yet, as I said, he did host the show once when I was on vacation. Maybe I should have sneaked back into the studio and walked on as a surprise guest.

Reggie positively belongs in the Hall of Fame. But when he is enshrined, don't look for me to be there, standing by live to interview Mr. Magnitude.

Jim Brown, in my opinion, is working harder than any athlete or former athlete in America, with the exception of what Arthur Ashe was doing, to affect positive change.

Of course, he's doing it his way, which is the same way he played football—angry, tough, knocking people down, never dancing out of bounds. He has never been in step, in line, or in anyone's control.

Jim Brown works on a principle best expressed by a former gang member who now works with him. The man's name is T, and he was explaining why Brown is so effective in his ghetto war.

"Power respects power," T said.

Occasionally Brown will let his wall down. I ran into him in San Francisco a few years ago. We decided to have lunch and we were walking through the city. We got onto the subject of the doo-wop singing groups of the Fifties and Sixties and Jim was telling me how much he loved that music when he was growing up.

I was a big doo-wop fan, too, and we started singing some of the old songs. We were strolling along the streets of San Francisco singing "Why Do Fools Fall in Love?" and other favorites.

But that's a side of his personality he does not often present to the public. Jim Brown is bad. Tough. Angry.

I think he likes to see himself as a lightning rod for trouble, the white establishment trying to bring him down because of his powerful opinions and ideas and personality.

He'll tell you that's why his problems with women have been publicly exaggerated, because everything he does is made to look bad. "I love women, I have great respect for women," he says, yet his actions and his words often prove otherwise. Tossing a woman off a balcony, for instance, is tough to chalk up to media persecution.

I don't think Jim is what you would call enlightened about women, although I know that he is now incorporating women into key roles in his gangbusting program.

I've known Brown several years and I like him a lot. He's been on the show probably a dozen times, starting when he was going through his male menopause, when he was talking about trying out for the Raiders at age fifty.

He always was a guy with impact, but I think right now he's the most effective he has ever been in his life. He is the founder and leader of The Amer-I-Can Program, an organization working to bust up inner city gangs, redirect goals, financially empower the people in the ghettos.

He does not do it by courting popular favor. One thing you never have to worry about with Jim Brown is that he will try to sweet-talk you. Example: Brown has publicly criticized Magic Johnson and Michael Jordan, accused them of trading their souls and their pride for money and popularity.

He said, "Jordan and Magic are modern-day versions of the old mulatto slaves who, because they had three or four drops of white blood, got preferential treatment. Isn't it characteristic of the house nigger to want to be just like the master?"

We discussed that on the show. I asked Brown if he really believes Jordan and Johnson are "house niggers."

"Well, yes," he said. "First of all, let me say that I like Magic. They are only representative, because they have the power and the money, it's not personal with Michael or Magic. I like all of those young men because basically they're very nice young men. But they have benefited from the blood of those who went before them.

"Those young men are not Muhammad Alis, they are not Paul Robesons, they are not Jackie Robinsons, in fact most of them don't even understand who most of those people were, and the fact that those people not only risked the money they could make, but they risked their lives. In the case of Paul Robeson, a broken man, because he stood up, he just did not do those things that the establishment wanted him to do, so that he would have a wonderful life for himself."

The contributions of Magic and Jordan, in your mind then, are not as valid as an Ali or Robeson, but they are considerable, would you not agree?

"No, they are very harmful, because the first thing is that we are looked upon as a culture, we are identified as black, we are put into a condition. Then some of us are used as role models to say that you can come out of that condition by being a gladiator and saying all the things that we want you to say, and you will be rich. But while you're rich, those ghettos out there are festering with the killing, the poverty, the oppression. The jails are overcrowded.

"If the system is correct, and Michael Jordan and Magic and those guys were doing the right thing, why are those ghettos becoming worse and worse?"

Then Brown surprised me, and one thing a true rebel never loses is the power to surprise. I asked him what his motivation is. What's in it for him? I expected him to give me some lofty speech about the good of society.

Here's what he said: "I can sit here with this man [T, the former gang member] and say this man loves me, even though he never played football with me, he never made a lot of money with me. We have young men out there who care about me more than anyone else. I need to be loved, and they love me for the same things that other people hate me for."

The true rebel rebels against being liked. So I guess that would make Bobby Knight the rebel's rebel, because I don't know anyone who works harder at being disliked than does Bobby

With me, he has succeeded. I know that by many measures, Knight is an enormously positive force. His players at Indiana U. graduate, they win championships and there is probably a real character-building element to his coaching style, even if the character is built simply by having survived a college basketball career under the whip of the terrible Bobby Knight.

Knight has never been on *Up Close,* but I made him a focal point of the show one day after he had ripped television for ruining college sports. The occasion of his tirade was an Indiana game that started late in the evening to accommodate an ESPN telecast.

I said, "While many of the criticisms of TV and its impact on sport are valid, Knight is off base here. For one thing, the start time was agreed upon by the conference and the school.

"Television, scourge of the American civilization as it is reputed to be, does fund intercollegiate athletics handsomely, and fuels the interest for those not lucky enough to attend in person.

"I'm not here to defend TV. Actually I'd like to take this opportunity to tell you about this principled, honorable protector of the student-athlete."

I mentioned Knight's chair tossing, the tirades, the fight with the cop at the Pan Am Games, the intimidation of the press and game officials, the treatment of his own players. I mentioned how he had treated Steve Alford, the quintessential All-American kid. Knight called Alford a little SOB, threw him out of numerous practices, blamed him for losing a game when he was suspended for participating in a charity fundraising project.

I went on: "I hear you say, 'That's part of Knight's brilliance. Testing his players' wills. Challenging their manhood.' Knight, you say, is also compassionate, generous and sentimental, even to strangers. Maybe so, but it's becoming evident that Knight is a man whose style is anathema to sport. His obsessions, his gracelessness, his joyless, compulsive behavior, is ugly and ruinous to the true qualities of the athletic life."

Duke coach Mike Krzyzewski presents an opposing viewpoint on Mr. Knight.

Krzyzewski played basketball at West Point under a young coach named Bobby Knight. Knight was a disciplinarian. To encourage point-guard Krzyzewski to be more pass-conscious, Knight told him, "If you shoot, I'll break your arm."

"And I believed him," Krzyzewski said. "I didn't shoot. I was probably his most disciplined player, because I was not dumb enough to do something that he did not want me to do.

"I think the thing a player does not like about any coach is if they try to extract from you what your potential is. There were days when you say, 'Hey, I'm not giving my potential today, no way.' And he says, 'Yes you are.' You say, 'Well, you can't make me do it,' and he says, 'I might have to do it in an extraordinary way.'

"When coach Knight did that with me, I didn't like it. Now I look back at it and say, 'Do I need to do it that way [with Duke players], or are there other ways I can do it?' You figure out ways within your own personality."

Krzyzewski told a West Point story. After a tough loss he was in a malt shop with a girl. Knight happened to walk past the malt shop. He saw his point-guard inside, laughing. Knight barged into the malt shop and told Krzyzewski that if he felt that good after a loss, maybe he shouldn't be on the team.

"Coach Knight has a great presence, and remember, he was in his twenties then. I'm not sure he would do it exactly that way now, but the message was a good message. You know what? I was ready for the next ballgame."

Knight's relationship with Krzyzewski went deeper than creative berating, though.

"My dad passed away when I was a senior," Krzyzewski said. "I was the captain of the basketball team. We had just beaten Navy and we were getting ready for a two-game trip, and all of a sudden he died. I was devastated.

"Coach Knight flew to Chicago and spent three days with my family, and made my mom feel at ease. He told me, 'You don't have to come back,' but I did, and we won the game and went on to the NIT. That's a side of coach Knight that people don't understand."

Remember the scene in *The Wild One?*

"What are you rebelling against?"

"Whataya got?"

That was Billy Martin, who spent his whole life with a chip on his shoulder and died with a six-pack on his lap.

Some rebel-type guys are creations of a media starved for color, but Billy was everything he was supposed to be and more. Truly a walking soap opera. He fought Reggie Jackson and he fought a marshmallow salesman, and you can't make stuff like that up.

My first interview with Billy Martin was in 1972 or 1973. I was about nineteen, it was one of my first shots at working in front of the camera. I approached him warily, as you did to just about all the Yankees of that era, but especially Billy.

Surprise. He was more friendly than a puppy dog. That's one thing about Billy, he could be one of the great charmers of all time. Also one of the great morose brooders and powder kegs.

Approaching Billy was like playing the lottery, but I was fortunate enough to mostly catch him on good days.

He was devoutly religious and had trouble with liquor and trouble with women and trouble with players and press and people in bars.

At one time he was married to two women at once. He had a daughter doing time in a South American prison on cocaine charges.

He came on the show not long after the incident in Arlington, Texas, where he got beat up in the men's room of a topless joint and tossed into the alley.

"I was beat up, Roy," he said, "I was beat up by three guys. If a sixty-year-old man was beat up, with any other name but Billy Martin, they would say it was a muggin', but bein's my name's Billy Martin . . ."

He did everything but whip out a harmonica and sing the blues.

The last interview I did with Billy was the year before he died in that car crash on Christmas night, on the way home from a liquor-store run.

Billy was telling me, "God loves me, Roy, God knows who Billy Martin is."

And almost in mid-sentence he stopped and said, "May I just do one thing, Roy? May I just say hello to all my deaf friends out there?"

He turned to the camera and made hand signs that said "Hello" and "I love you," then turned back to me and went on talking.

I think Robert DeNiro would be a knockout playing the title role in *The Billy Martin Story*.

We may be looking at the end of an era in tennis, folks: The end of Tantrum Tennis. The end of R-rated, sneering, posturing, pouting, whining, bullying, blow-top American tennis.

Unless Andrew Dice Clay takes up the sport, it looks like we've come to the end of a line. If so, let this serve as a fond farewell salute to two guys who did so much to enliven the game over the last two decades—John McEnroe and Jimmy Connors. And a non-farewell salute to the kid many thought would carry on the tradition, but has turned into a nice guy—Andre Agassi.

Despite Agassi's promising start as a crybaby hothead, I realized one day he had no chance to carry on that tradition. We got together for dinner one night in Las Vagas, we were talking music and I asked Mr. Rock 'n' Roll Tennis who he liked to listen to.

I figured maybe Whitesnake. The Dead Kennedys. Or maybe something louder and darker.

"Barry Manilow is my favorite," he said.

I swear. He showed me the cassettes in his car to prove it.

I learned other tawdry details of Andre's life. He loves his parents, is faithful to his longtime girlfriend, has maintained the same circle of friends for years, is never rude to strangers. His favorite restaurant is a truck stop.

His first few years on the tour he showed a lot of promise. He would tank matches, quit, choke, cry and whine. Long hair and short fuse. A prima donna.

Of course, psychologists recognize this as normal teenage behavior. While sponsors were trying to build his rebel image, Andre was growing out of it, maturing, and becoming a for-real tennis player.

I went to an exhibition match in Los Angeles a year or so ago, Agassi vs. McEnroe. Because the pros play year 'round, there is always the danger in an exhibition match between two big names that they will fall asleep in midpoint.

But there was Agassi, grunting and sweating, hair and jewelry flying, kicking McEnroe's butt.

And there was McEnroe, swearing, throwing his racket ten times, emoting like Hamlet after every point.

People keep waiting for McEnroe to mature, to outgrow his anger and his bad manners, but it will never happen.

His act is more than an act, it's an essential part of his genius. He has to work himself into a near hysteria to play his best. I remember an old Superman adventure, where Superman somehow was split into two Supermen and he had to battle himself.

That's McEnroe. He admitted to me that on the court he is his own worst enemy, and needs to be.

He represents the best and worst of an American athlete. Arrogant, hostile, rude, profane. And yet tough, brash, bold, daring, colorful.

Short fuse? How about no fuse? You wouldn't be surprised if McEnroe threw a racquet losing the service flip.

Yet his greatness can't be denied.

John is a terrific guest, because he holds nothing back. He's as honest and up front on camera as he is on the court.

A sampling:

On his wife, Tatum O'Neal (from whom he is separated at the time of this writing): "She's a female John McEnroe. We have very similar personalities. She's a very strong personality."

On Boris Becker: "Boris, as hard as I've tried to dislike him for competitive reasons, he's turned out to be a nice kid."

On Jimmy Connors, whom he called a phony: "Well, I mean Jimmy is very good at playing the [corporate sponsorship] game now, he's learned how to do that. Also, he loves the sport so much that he wants to be around it, whereas I don't really feel the same way in the sense that I have to be extra nice to certain sponsors.

"But he and I get along better than we ever have. We dine together, we have respect for each other. It's a hell of a lot easier when you're off the court."

McEnroe told about a match against Ivan Lendl.

"We were playing an exhibition in Italy about seven years ago. There were ten thousand people there and he was giving no effort whatsoever. I was thinking, 'This is crazy, this is going to hurt the exhibitions.' So I started yelling obscene things to him, telling him he's a chicken, he shouldn't be allowed to do this, it's a waste of my time.

"I won the first set 6-1 and was up one-love in the second when I started getting on him. I promise you, I've never seen him try the way he tried the rest of that set. He wound up beating me that set, and 6-4 in the third, and after that he beat me seven straight matches.

"I hurt myself there. See? I bring out the best and worst in people. The funny thing was, people ended up booing me at the end of the match, because I lost after being ahead. I don't know how I ended up getting the short end of that stick, but I did."

I caught Jimmy Connors's act when I was starting in the TV business in Miami. I remember being courtside with my camera crew at a Connors match, and Jimbo was screaming and cursing at us, the filthiest, dirtiest language you can imagine.

He has the best sneer in tennis. Maybe in any sport. And a great inner fire. Some of that may have come from the way he was raised. He grew up in East St. Louis, Illinois, a tough town, and his mother, while pregnant with Jimmy, literally bulldozed a court in the backyard to keep Jimmy and his brother off the streets.

He was coached by his mother and grandmother, but insists that it wasn't a mama's boy image he has always fought against.

"Back where I came from," he said, "it was a little bit weird to run around in a little pair of white shorts, and that was the abuse that I took."

And when he started venturing across the Mississippi River to the nicer courts in St. Louis, Missouri, he was treated like a dirty street kid. Maybe that's why his game came to incorporate the crotch-grabbing, bird-flipping and obscenity-spewing. He would win because he was meaner, tougher and nastier than the other guy.

"My attitude toward my game is something that was inside me, and it took my mom and grandmother to pull that out of me," he said. "Maybe they pulled it a little too far."

Maybe, but it has helped make for a great run of bad-boy tennis.

Spike Lee is the only guest we ever had to pay to get on the show.

I probably shouldn't mention it, I don't want to give people ideas, but Spike agreed to come on the show only if we got him two free tickets to the 1990 Super Bowl.

Spike is a major sports fan, a rebel filmmaker, and a guy who can find racial overtones in just about everything.

We were talking about a comment by John Salley, about how Salley feels it important to put his money back into the black community, as Malcolm X suggested years ago.

"I was talking to Kareem about this," Lee said. "There's not a collective group of black people in America that makes as much money as black athletes, and if more of them thought like John did . . .

"Most of these guys, they don't read, they're ignorant, all they care about is how much money they're gonna make and how many women they're gonna bone.

"And *Sports Illustrated* putting that bum on the cover, what's his name."

I don't know. Which bum?
"On the Atlanta Falcons."

Deion Sanders.
"Deion! He should be shot. That guy, he's gonna get a knee injury, another two years he's gonna be a bum on the street."

But isn't that about democracy, that a guy can be—
"But why they gotta promote somebody like that?"

Because it's a democracy.
"Twenty pounds of gold around his neck.

Because it's a democracy, Spike.

"Jheri curls drippin' down the back of his shirt."

But we're all different . . .

"All I'm sayin' is it's no mistake that that's what they're pushin'."

Seven months later, Prime Time himself came on the show. It was Deion Sanders's chance to defend himself against some of the criticism leveled at him for his unique style and his ambitious two-sport career. I guess Deion surprised me with the gentlemanly way he chose not to lash out at people who bad-mouthed him. Except for Spike Lee, of course.

Now you're going to have a chance to answer the critics today, and I know this is something you've wanted to do for some time.

"Very much."

Let's start off with your friend and mine, Spike Lee.

"Oh, this is a good one! I can't wait for this one."

Spike was on our show several months back and he lit into, not just you, but all the guys who are showy and flamboyant and flashy.

(Here we played the clip of Spike's trashing of Sanders.)

Wait a minute, there's no Jheri curl juice dripping down your back, Deion.

"No, man, Spike, man, he's a little 150-pound Jiminy Cricket-lookin' entertainer-director you have on your show and he's supposed to be the authority on—"

Jiminy Cricket?

"Jiminy Cricket, and he's supposed to be the expert on black athletes in today's society, and that really hurts me, because Spike Lee's a black man, talkin' about another black man on national television."

But let's be honest now. This is not the first time blacks have criticized you. In fact I'm going to read you a quote that was in the Atlanta Constitution, *by Chet Fuller, a black writer: ''Sickeningly glorifying the flashy, quick-success, easy-money lifestyle of those who cheat thousands of young kids who hang on their every word and can't wait for the day when they, too, sign a multimillion-dollar contract and have their chests gold-plated.''*

"Well, I don't know if Chet or Spike Lee grew up in my community, where we had all the drug dealers with all the gold chains and all the big, fancy cars, and the children in my community looked up to all those guys. So why can't I do the same thing, without the drugs, in a positive atmosphere, and show the kids there's another way out—with education and school and sports?"

(We showed a video of Sanders scoring a touchdown and celebrating with a dancelike kick.)

"That kick there, that's something my mother and my girl love to death, and I do it for them. I work hard all week long, and I been workin' hard for sixteen years to be a professional athlete, and once I get loose, I think I should be able to do whatever I would like to do."

Are you an athlete, or are you an entertainer, a showman?

"I'm not only an athlete. Prime Time is an entertainer, also. The fans pay fifteen or twenty dollars a ticket, they don't want to see the old days, people just knockin' each other's heads off, run in to score and throw the ball back to the referee. I like to give 'em some extra. I like for 'em to go home and say, 'Did you see the way Prime Time worked them boys over?' "

(We played a clip from sportswriter Ralph Wiley.)

Wiley: "Half of being a great athlete is applying your mind to what you're doing, and Deion's got a four-three body in a five-flat mind."

Sanders: "Four-three body in a five-flat mind? Who was that? What's important to me is getting my mother off two jobs she worked all her life, and so I could dress this way and look this way, and I was able to do so.

"And when I was going into the NFL, defensive backs wasn't on the high money scale, so if you created something different, like Prime Time, that puts you up on the scale."

Before we go any further, if you see Spike Lee, what did you just tell me, off the air, you might want to try to do to him?

"I might want to just hit him in the chest and let his body curl around my fist. No, I don't mean no harm on Spike. I wish him well, but it really hurts me for him to sit on television and talk about me.

"If you really listen to Deion Sanders, he never criticizes anyone else, he talked about himself in college, to get to the professional level. Once I accomplished my goal, the show was over, the thrill was gone, and now I'm just a regular Deion."

Is it money that you're after with all the hype? Jim McMahon, I think you said that he wasn't the best quarterback in the world, but nobody made ten million faster than Jim McMahon.

"That was important to me, being something other than just a defensive back. I wanted to be the best defensive back, I wanted to be the most-known defensive back, I wanted to be a star."

I was told that you're a quiet guy. Bo Jackson has ripped you, but you've never ripped back at Bo?

"I don't get into that, I don't talk about other people, unless they just get like Spike Lee. But Bo Jackson is a great athlete and I wish him the best of luck. I would never retaliate like that, because God don't like ugly. And I think a man who will put another man down is a man that won't go anywhere."

I think the meanest shot was Lester Hayes, a guy you idolized as a kid. Lester says, "Deion got his rep chasin' down Caucasian Clydesdales, and his destiny is to spend time in a pen."

"But see, I received a letter from Lester the next week and he said that reporters turned the whole thing around, and he admires me, and I told him I loved him to death, I wear his T-shirt under my uniform every game."

You feel like you're your own man, and you'll be respected as a person.

"Every time when I go to sleep at night, and wake up in the morning and look in the mirror, I see somebody who is real. I don't live a lie, I tell it just like it is."

I was impressed with Sanders, because he showed a more serious side, a more thoughtful side than most of us are used to seeing.

And maybe that really is the new Deion. However, since then, we've seen Deion in a less flattering role: Deion as nemesis of the media.

After the deciding game of the 1992 National League playoffs, as his delirious Atlanta Braves teammates were celebrating the most dramatic baseball win in recent memory, Sanders was a one-man bucket brigade, dousing broadcaster Tim McCarver with ice water several times because McCarver had dared to question Sanders's commitment to his team.

What McCarver should have said when Deion tossed the water, was "See what I mean, folks?"

During the Series, Deion refused to talk to the media, although he was a key member of the team.

And in football, even if you love the touchdown dance, how lovable is it when Deion trips the light fantastic after scoring a touchdown when his team is down by thirty-eight points?

Muhammad Ali's famous poem, "Me, whee!", could apply to Deion, except that Ali never hurt anyone, never hated even his toughest critics, never forgot that it was all just a game.

What Deion seems to have lost somewhere along the line is his sense of humor. Maybe it got lost in his sense of importance, or in the avalanche of self-promotion tinged with paranoia.

I'm not saying Deion should be more humble or more lovable, so that Middle America can embrace him. But the importance of selling shoes and selling the image and the Magnitude of Deion seems to have wiped out Sanders's ability to be a human being, too.

He became the poster child for the Me Generation. Don't just keep up with the Joneses, but kick the Joneses' ass.

Not that it's all Deion's fault, and he's not the only character showing signs of losing touch with reality. As sports fans, we congratulate and marvel and gawk and fawn and forgive, and we feed the monster.

Anyway, maybe Deion will come back on the show and defend himself against yet another media critic—me. I want to be a Prime Time fan, but he has been making it tough.

As I signed off the air on that show, Deion said, "We gonna stay cool. Hi to Spike."

About a year later I ran into Spike at a banquet and he said, "Hey, you gotta stop playing that tape."

What tape?
"The tape of me talkin' about Deion."
(I had used that bite in a year-end highlights show.)

Why?
"Because me and Deion are tight now."

Great. Why don't you come on the show and set the record straight? Everyone has already seen the clip, not showing it isn't going to let people know how you feel now.
"No, man, I just want you to stop playin' the tape. Me and Deion are straight now."

Apparently someone convinced Deion that I had goaded Spike into insulting and attacking Deion on the show, and Deion, being the forgiving guy he is, had forgiven Jiminy Cricket.

TWELVE

THE CIRCUS
AND THE
PARTY

"It's been a good 'un."

—DON MEREDITH, TO A FRANTIC FELLOW
PASSENGER WHEN IT APPEARED THAT THEIR
JET AIRLINER WAS GOING TO CRASH.

I was on my way to South Carolina for a personal appearance and had to change planes in Atlanta. It's a huge airport, you walk forever.

As soon as I got off the plane it struck me that something was not quite right. The airport was very quiet, and even though there were a lot of people, there didn't seem to be the usual airport bustle.

People were jammed together in front of the TV sets in the little cocktail lounges, as if they were watching a big game, but by the stunned silence I knew it was something bad.

My first thought was that the President had been shot. I stopped at one gathering and stared over the tops of a hundred heads at the TV screen. A man in a suit was speaking at a press conference. I heard him giving medical information, yet there didn't seem to be an urgency or panic.

Just then a guy in the crowd watching the television recognized me and said, "Hey, Roy Firestone. Did you hear? Magic Johnson has AIDS."

For a moment I couldn't speak, or even move. My feet went numb and I couldn't get my bearings, like when you're having a bad dream and you aren't in control of your thinking processes.

This is not to say that Magic's announcement about having the HIV virus shocked or stunned me more than the next guy because I'm such a sensitive person or such close buddies with Magic. The shock was universal.

But so much of what I do—my career, my life, why I'm in the business I'm in—is wrapped up in people like Magic Johnson. To oversimplify, I went into TV sports journalism because I was fascinated by the Magics and I wanted to find out what makes them so special.

I've had the opportunity to get to know and spend time with the two athletes who stand above the rest in terms of a certain personal magic—Earvin Johnson and Muhammad Ali. They're the rare type of people who when you get to know them don't change the way you feel about them as much as they change the way you feel about yourself.

Not that they are perfect. Both Ali and Magic have been beset by sizable personal problems of their own making, and both have life-threatening health problems that almost certainly could have been avoided had they heeded reasonable advice. Both, held to higher standards, have failed on some counts to live up to those standards.

Heroes? In a sense they are, and in a sense they most definitely are not. Yet they strutted their hour upon the stage and lit it up like no other athletes of this half century.

It seems ironic that both of them are making their exits from the stage in a tragic manner so at odds with the joy they brought to their athletic gifts and personalities.

Not that either Ali or Magic is treating his illness as a tragedy. Quite the opposite. Both have avoided self-pity, neither has retreated from public view. It's the Don Meredith philosophy, I guess, the outlook of the lucky few who have enjoyed an ultimate ride but always knew it wouldn't last forever.

If Magic and Ali aren't going to mope, who are we to do it for them? As Karl "Mailman" Malone said when Magic retired for the final time from the NBA, "I don't want to say I feel sorry for Magic, because Magic don't want no one to feel sorry for him."

Consider this, then, a thank-you note to the two guys who, more than anyone else in sports, have made it a good 'un for me.

My very first day as a sports anchor on WPLG-TV in Miami in 1978, I was assigned to take my crew to the airport to interview the heavyweight champion of the world.

Ali's career really got started in Miami, at the old Fifth Street Gym with Angelo Dundee and Dr. Ferdie Pacheco. But he had moved to Chicago, and now he was flying to Miami to train for a fight with Ken Norton.

Ali was thirty-six years old at the time, no longer lean and hungry, although his career would drag on for another four years.

I had seen the Ali act many times before at the Fifth Street Gym, and was expecting more of the same—poetry, brash predictions, playful bombast and mugging, the patented Ali monologue that puts to shame all the boxers before and after him, not to mention all the professional wrestlers.

Instead, the Ali getting off the plane was a somewhat plump, weary-looking man in a business suit. He was gracious about doing the interview, as always, but his eyes weren't bright and he spoke slowly and quietly, as if he were drowsy.

One question I asked him was why he kept boxing, well past what most consider to be a boxer's prime.

"So many people all over the world want to see the champ," he said. "I'm not just the champ of America, I'm the champ of Africa, of South America, of Russia and Europe. I'm the people's champ."

He mumbled and rambled and after about five minutes he was really winding down, the interview was just about over. Then he said, "What did you say your name was?"

I told him, and he said, "Boy! You callin' me boy?"

"No, *Roy.*"

"My name's not boy, Roy. Who you callin' Roy? Why, I oughta whup you . . ."

He went into a little routine he's done a thousand times with a thousand reporters, where he feigns anger, puts up his dukes, wants to fight. Suddenly, like a switch was flipped, he came to life. His eyes brightened, his voice became lively. With me playing the straight man, he did about a minute of his rap, and no matter how many times you've seen him do it, there's no way you can't laugh or smile.

And then he was gone. That night on the news I used only the good stuff, not the sad stuff. Now, looking back, I see that he wasn't jet-lagged, or tired from training, but that this was the beginning of the end for Ali.

Over the years I talked to him from time to time, I'd see him at fights and he was always friendly. One encounter was especially memorable for me.

In my stand-up act I have a video of Ali's career and life, along with which I sing Simon and Garfunkel's "The Boxer," but I've changed the lyrics to make it a tribute to Ali.

I was playing at a sports memorabilia convention in 1990. Ali was due in town to be an honored guest the following night, so as I started into "The Boxer," I looked out over the audience, thinking he might have come in early and I could introduce him, but he wasn't there.

My version of the song ends with a soaring reprise. I sing of Ali as an older man, and it's very sentimental. I got a nice round of applause. Then, in a strange, delayed reaction, people started standing and cheering.

I turned and there, right behind me on the stage, was Ali. He hugged me and said, "Tonight made me feel special."

It was nice, for one small moment, to return that favor. It was the single greatest moment I've ever had performing.

In a movie about Ali's life, I have a bit part, a reporter interviewing the champ. Ironically, I've never interviewed him on the show.

I did get him to agree to be a guest on *Up Close* a few years ago. I knew he might be hard to understand, and slow, but I also knew the viewers would understand, and it would allow them to see that Ali, while down, isn't out, that the spirit is still there.

But Ali had a last-minute change of heart. He was working on his biography with a writer named Tom Hauser, and Ali told

Hauser to relay to me that he didn't want to come on the show because he felt like he couldn't be himself.

So Hauser came on and talked about Ali. He told about going with the champ to visit some kids in a cerebral palsy ward. No photographers, no hype. Ali is a complete and total pushover for kids. When the visit was over, Ali hugged each of the children and kissed each on the lips.

Hauser told of Ali hearing of a Jewish old-folks home in New York that would be torn down, leaving the old people homeless. Quietly, Ali bankrolled a new home.

When it was finished he went to visit. In one corner of the room was a very old man, by himself. Ali approached the man and did the mock fight thing with his fists.

The man's face brightened. Bundini Brown, Ali's trainer, said to the old man, "Do you know who this is?"

And the old man said, "Yeah, it's the champ!"

"That's right," Brown said.

The old man said, "I know him, he's the greatest, he's Joe Louie!"

Everyone chuckled, and Brown started to correct the old man, to tell him who this really was.

Ali stopped Brown, whispered to him, "If it makes him happy to meet Joe Louis, if that's who his hero was, let's not confuse him."

Ali earned people's respect, but from those around him, more than anything, he earned their affection. Their love.

Like Angelo Dundee, who trained eleven boxing champions, but had a special attachment to Ali. Angelo was on the show, and I asked him if Ali was a victim of the sport.

"Naaaa. Ali did what he wanted to do, Ali's a very happy individual. Ali's the type of individual would be happy with one car, one suit."

You had no regrets then, in okaying fights late in his career, like the Holmes fight, like the Berbick fight, now knowing that he might have suffered some damage?

"I appreciate you giving me that compliment. I never had to okay anything, because the manager did that. But the fights I okayed, I felt he could win. I thought he could beat Larry Holmes, and I still think he could've if he hadn't taken those [diet] pills to make himself look svelte, so he'd look pretty in front of a mirror, the pretty body. He was empty that night."

We showed some old photos of Ali and had Angelo narrate, talk us down memory lane.

"What can you say? I met this guy when he was a young kid, I met him when he was sixteen, he told me he was going to win the Olympics, that was two years before the Olympics.

"He's a joy to be with. The thing about working with fighters, it's a fun trip, you bounce off each other, it's rapport. Like Drew Brown, very important in Ali's life. They called those guys Ali's entourage. I didn't like that. Everybody with Muhammad Ali was important.

"Even training was fun. He worked harder than any fighter, ever. First in the gym, last out. He would run from downtown Miami to the Fifth Street Gym.

"He changed boxing. He was the most available superstar of our time. Great man, I love him because he taught me patience, and to be nice."

Dr. Ferdie Pacheco met Ali when he was training in Miami and Ferdie was a doctor in the ghetto, also serving the fighters at Fifth Street Gym. They became friends and remained close over the years. Ferdie loves to talk about Ali.

"He was so exceptional in the beginning," Pacheco said on one of his appearances on the show. "When he walked into my office the first time, I think he'd had two professional fights and he was babbling about being the greatest of all time. When he left, my nurse, Miss Mabel Norwood, turns to me and says, 'Either that child is a fool, or he *is* going to be the next heavyweight champion of the world.'

"He loved to box. He wasn't a brutal fighter, except against Floyd Patterson and Ernie Terrell, because they wouldn't call him Ali. He strung those fights out.

"Outside of those two fights, you didn't see the element of anger in any of his fights. Even against Joe Frazier, he was just in there to do the best he could. Frazier was mad, Muhammad wasn't. And he couldn't understand why anyone would be mad at him after the fight.

"Ali had the sweetest mother that ever lived. She was soft and wonderful and yielding. So he hated to hurt people, hated to cause confrontations. His father was a painter and singer who was held down because he was a black man in Louisville. He was a racist of the worst kind and tried to instill distrust in his son.

"Ali hated to get embarrassed. He would not go in a place and say, 'Serve me, I'm the heavyweight champion of the world.' I remember the time we took a bus from Miami all the way up to Lewiston, Maine, we had Ed Pope of the Miami *Herald* with us, and a *Sports Illustrated* writer. The only guy that would get out and challenge at every bus stop was Bundini. He'd get thrown out of every bus stop, and Ali thought it was the funniest thing he ever saw. Ali never got out of the bus. He said, 'Bring a sandwich into the bus,' because he was like Odessa (his mother).

"Remember the old Johnny Mercer song, 'You have to accentuate the positive, eliminate the negative, don't mess with Mr. In Between'? Well that was this guy's whole career. Even today, Ali serves a function. By example, he shows people that are sick with serious illnesses how to cope. He has great serenity, peace of mind. His feeling is, 'Look, these are the cards I've been dealt, these are the cards I'm going to play.' "

The circus continues, though at a much slower pace. Parkinson's disease has taken a toll, and I'm convinced a lot of Ali's current state is just utter fatigue, the result of leading that Ali circus around the world for so many years, carrying so many people on his shoulders, financially and spiritually.

He's still an amazing guy. For all of Ali's great bombast and global personality and warrior-like ring dominance and good looks, what stands out above all else is his kindness, of which he still seems to have an unlimited supply.

Even his run-ins had an Ali-like humor. Like when a flight attendant asked him to fasten his seat belt.

"Superman don't need no seat belt," he said.

"Superman don't need no airplane," she said.

I remember the time in Los Angeles when Ali somehow was summoned to the scene of a suicide attempt, a man threatening to leap from a freeway overpass. He picked up a megaphone and said something like, "This is Ali! You can't jump, I need you, champ! You gonna jump, you gotta come down here and whup me first!"

Ali was already afflicted with Parkinson's disease, but he summoned up enough of the old magic to talk the man down.

The most powerful force in life is the power of kindness, and Ali is an enormously powerful man. I covered him since 1973, a good eight years of his career, and so many times I saw him work a room like no other person I've seen. Make everyone feel important.

Around Christmas time in 1991 I got a phone call from a friend of mine who does promotional work for Ali and knows I'm a big Ali fan. He said Muhammad was in town, would I like to come over and just hang with him at his hotel while he did some work?

I went to Ali's hotel room, and it was a surreal scene. The room was packed to the ceiling with boxing gloves, thousands of big fat leather gloves. His job was to autograph each pair of gloves, to be sold by Sears in their sports memorabilia catalogue.

He signed each glove slowly and meticulously, and we watched a football game on TV. Ali loves magic, so his people hired a magician to come in and do some tricks to keep Muhammad alert and focused on his task.

Ali performed some of his own magic tricks, and he's pretty good, but he's like an enthusiastic kid who's learning the tricks and is still kind of clumsy.

We talked some, and I did a little bit of a Howard Cosell impersonation, Howard as a rapper announcing an Ali fight. Ali loved it, although his reactions were on about a thirty-second delay.

Three times during the day he got up and went in another room to kneel and pray to Mecca.

He was subdued and quiet the whole time, but he seemed to be enjoying himself. He never showed an ounce of cynicism, never seemed bored, never rude. He made me feel completely welcome, and I know he's done the same thing a thousand times over the years with thousands of people he barely knows.

At one point he started telling me about a comeback he was planning, an exhibition bout in Tunisia to raise funds for a Muslim school in Chicago. The man can barely walk and talk, yet he was going on and on about how he would fight Holyfield and Tyson.

"We're gonna get Tyson out of jail, we're gonna fight and raise money for this charity."

He was serious, and it was absurd and sad, but after about ten minutes I started believing.

"You watch! Tunisia is gonna pay me fifty million dollars to fight! I'm gonna fight Holyfield for fifty million dollars! And I'm gonna get the money for the children in Chicago."

What could be sadder than the former champion, already so damaged by his sport, sitting in a hotel room signing boxing gloves for sale and talking about making a comeback?

And yet there was no sadness. You can't hang around Ali and feel anything but good. Even though I've been in the outer rings, it's been great fun to be a part of the circus.

If Ali led the circus, Magic Johnson threw the party.

"Party," of course, carries tragic connotations in a discussion of Magic now. But the party extended far beyond the busy romantic life of Magic's bachelor days. It encompassed his basketball playing and his whole life. On one of his appearances on the show, before the 1990–1991 season, he talked about the party.

"Life for Earvin Johnson—or I should say, Magic Johnson—is one big party. Because even before all this [success] happened to me, I had so much fun.

"Back in sixth and seventh grade, hanging out on street corners, singing, playing hide-and-go-seek, doin' all those things, I had a good time. Workin' at the Boys' Club, workin' for Big Brother/Big Sister, workin' at the grocery store, the corner store, I had a good time. I had fun.

"And still, in all that's comin' I'm having fun, and three years from now when all this [basketball] is gone and past me, I'm going to still be having fun, and fifty years from now I'm going to be having fun.

"My motto is this: Just wake up and have a good day, have a good time, and no matter what goes wrong, turn that into something good. Still come out smiling, still come out having a good time. People look and say, 'That's not real.' Hey, I'm havin' fun. I'm havin' fun because life is too short not to enjoy it."

A shallow philosophy? Well, as George Santayana said, "There is no cure for birth and death save to enjoy the interval."

Which is what Magic is still doing, even though the HIV virus put him out of basketball two years ahead of schedule and added several layers of turmoil and controversy to his life.

I was there at the beginning of the party, at least the pro basketball portion of it. It was NBA draft day in 1979 and me and my KCBS-TV crew were filming a coin flip to decide whether the Bulls or Lakers would draft first.

Actually the coin was flipped in New York, with both teams on a conference call. We were at the Forum, in the office of Jack Kent Cooke, then the owner of the Lakers.

Significantly, there was no national TV coverage of the NBA draft back then. That quiet era of NBA basketball was about to come to a close, with the events of that very day.

The Lakers were to make the heads/tails call. Chick Hearn, team broadcaster and assistant general manager, crossed his fingers and told NBA commissioner, Larry O'Brien, "Heads."

"It's heads," the commissioner said over the phone.

The party began. The Laker contingent went wild. Although at least one key Cooke advisor was urging him to draft Sidney Moncrief of Arkansas, Cooke knew who he wanted. He drafted Earvin Magic Johnson, a 19-year-old sophomore from Michigan State.

The Bulls took David Greenwood.

Ah, fate.

Cooke was about to sell his team and arena to Jerry Buss, but he wanted to leave behind something to be remembered by. Magic was that legacy.

"How do you feel, Mr. Cooke?" I asked him.

"Roy," Cooke said in his dramatic, stentorian tones, "Magic Johnson says it all, doesn't it?"

It did, and does, and man, it was a wild decade.

Magic took about five minutes to adjust to the spotlight of the NBA and the big city. I remember a game very early in that first season when he was the guest on the Lakers' postgame radio show.

The interviews were conducted at midcourt, with the sound piped over the PA system for the benefit of any fans who cared to hang around.

Magic turned the interview into a tent revival. He took the mike and spoke directly to the crowd.

"I know you fans pay your money, you want to see a show, right? You pay your five dollars, right? Your ten dollars, right? Your twenty dollars!"

And the fans were shouting back. "Yes! That's right, Magic!" And Magic was urging them on. Never before or since have I seen a player in a similar situation even acknowledge the fans, let alone play to them and involve them in the interview. I was half-expecting Magic to ask the sinners to come down and be saved.

He was some kid. He led the singing on the team bus, and he took charge of the team on the court, with heavy deference to Kareem Abdul-Jabbar. You couldn't compliment Magic on a necktie without him somehow deflecting the praise to Kareem: "Thank you, it is a nice tie, but you know, I wouldn't be able to shop for such fine neckties if it wasn't for Kareem and what he does for this team."

That's an exaggeration, but you would never, down through the years, catch Magic accepting the full glory for any moment, or for the decade of Showtime.

I remember in his rookie season, spending an afternoon at his apartment in Fox Hills near the Forum, doing a long interview.

It was a dinky apartment, decorated in Early Sophomore. Rented furniture, beanbag chairs, a cheap TV, a tiny refrigerator stocked with old pizza and a couple cans of soda pop.

But the apartment seemed to be the nerve center of Los Angeles. Every three minutes or so his intercom would sound, another visitor here to see Magic. The phone rang nonstop.

And music. Always music. The stereo was constantly on, and he would put on his headphones and announce the songs in the voice of E.J. the Deejay, then cackle and sing along in a voice that will never win him a Grammy. We'd be talking and he would break into a song.

He moved to nicer places, and a few years later he moved into his own big home in an exclusive, gated neighborhood in Bel Air. He invited me to bring my camera crew and take a tour of the Magic castle.

It was like a scene from a *Home Alone* movie, where the kid suddenly discovers that this is all his! The swimming pool, the upstairs disco/music room connecting to an indoor basketball court, the game room, the kitchen with more gadgets and controls than a 747 cockpit.

"I just never thought I would ever live in a house like this," he said. "It's like a dream."

Magic told me there was a young boy who lived next door who would come over, knock on the door and ask the housekeeper if Magic could play. And Magic would shoot hoops with the kid.

He led us into the dining room and sat down at the head of the huge table which had ten or twelve chairs. For a moment, it seemed, he forgot the camera and he began to have an imaginary dinner with his entire family. He had places for each brother and sister, and he pantomimed the meal.

"Here's the turkey for you, Mom, and would you please pass the potatoes, Dad?"

Well, that was two houses ago. Now he's building a mansion in the hills above Los Angeles, one of those mall-sized celebrity estates. I hope he enjoys it half as much as he did his first apartment.

One thing that hasn't changed, through the rise and end of Magic's career, through the changes in his life, is the smile. Every athlete has a stamp—Jordan at the buzzer, Reggie with two on and two out, Mays losing his cap. Magic's signature, to me, is the smile.

It doesn't turn off when the cameras do. After a game, night after night, icing his ankles and knees and shoulders and whatever else was aching, he would sit at his locker until long after the other Lakers had dressed and left, until only a few stragglers remained to ask the last questions or just hang a few minutes with Magic.

Sometimes he would fall back on clichéd answers, because the season itself, one hundred games plus, sometimes is a cliché. But often, if he could see someone taking the time to try to understand, Magic would take you deeper into his game and his heart.

The game was never so bad, his mood never so down that he would dress and dash out to avoid the press. He had time for the people who cared about him and who cared about basketball as much as he does.

I saw the routine a thousand times. Usually there would be a little kid or two, hanging back with his father, waiting for a chance to approach Magic when the crowd around his locker thinned. It was almost like visiting Santa Claus. Magic would sign an autograph, shake the kid's hand, ask him a question or two, share a laugh. If it was a small child, Magic would pick him up and talk to him eye-to-eye.

Then he would be off into the night, the party that swirled about him to be continued somewhere else.

That's why when the HIV news hit, it was like a member of my family being stricken, a member of all our families. If we can be like Magic for a moment and look for the good side of the bad news, I think that for at least a little while, Magic's sad announcement allowed us all to become closer by sharing a sense of mortality through a common friend, and by sharing his spirit.

If one moment symbolized that spirit, it is the 1992 NBA All-Star Game in Orlando. Magic Johnson was under siege. His own Laker teammates were saying he should not be allowed to play, since he had already retired. Newspaper polls showed a solid majority of fans in certain cities opposed to his participation. Players like Barkley and Jordan grumbled that with Magic in town, the game would become a Magic media circus.

But the fans had voted Magic in, and he said the hell with it, I'm playing. The only All-Star who really seemed to understand was Tim Hardaway, who would have been the starting point guard had Magic stayed home. Hardaway willingly stepped out of the starting lineup and said he was proud to do so.

Magic's friends and supporters were hoping he wouldn't be so rusty that he would embarrass himself. He didn't. He had what was, under the circumstances, the game of his life, capping it with a three-point bomb over Isiah Thomas at the buzzer.

It would have been nice for him to play the 1992–1993 season, take a victory lap around the league, but you can't say Magic got cheated out of a career. He led the Lakers to the NBA finals eight times and they won it all five times. He told me that after the final game of each championship, he went home by himself and cried.

"I want to be a winner," he said on the show. "It's not just on the basketball court, it's checkers, it's softball, it's basketball with my son or my sister. It doesn't matter. I don't know where and why it's in me, but it's just in me, and when I hit that floor, if I'm at practice or if I just pick up a game of cards with the guys, I want to win.

"I'm not a sore loser or a bad loser, but I'm a frustrated loser 'cause I want to figure out what happened and I want to make sure it don't happen again. That's what keeps me goin', just wanting to win. I won at every level—fourth grade, fifth, sixth, seventh, eighth, ninth, tenth, eleventh, twelfth, college, pro, and I'm used to it, so I want it some more, you know?

"When you hit that locker room and you see your suit hanging there, you lay back and you say, 'Wow, I'm here.' The excitement and thrill of the crowd, that chill just runs through your body and it's an unbelievable feeling. I love my work."

On that show in 1990, I asked him then about a rumor that he would play just one more season, 1990–1991, then retire.

"I'm gonna give you 'til my contract ends, that's three years," he said, "and that'll be it. I can't complain even if I left tomorrow, I've had a tremendous time, so much fun, so much excitement. Three years after this, that'll be it."

I asked him to describe the decade-long run known as Showtime.

"It was just a big party," he said. "It was just like undescribable. We were so close and we were so confident. We knew when we hit the floor we were the best team and we were out to prove that.

"But I think the best thing we had was we gave whatever it took to win. And when we stepped into that locker room, all those twelve egos was left outside, and we didn't care about money, we didn't care about nothin' else but just winnin', and doin' your job.

"Kareem didn't say a lot, he led by example. Norman (Nixon), Jamaal (Wilkes), (Jim) Chones, (Mark) Landsberger, (Brad) Holland, everybody, just did their job. Coop (Michael Cooper). We played basketball, but we played it on instinct. We went out and played. We just played ball. Most people were playin' *at* it, but we were playin' it.

"Now that all those guys are gone and I'm still sittin' here, I'm wonderin' what the Nineties are gonna be like."

THIRTEEN

TRUE
COLORS

I got a letter not long ago. "Dear Roy: Love your show, but enough's enough on the race stuff."

That person isn't alone. I hear it occasionally: Hey, it's a sports show! Sports is our island of refuge in the sea of human turmoil, where we go to escape the crummy problems of the real world.

I don't buy it. The problems of sport are just as real as the problems of the outside world. If there is racial discrimination in sport, for instance, do we ignore it because it gets in the way of our enjoyment of the Sunday football game?

The "race stuff" won't be wished away.

When Los Angeles was burning in the Spring of 1992 in the wake of the Rodney King verdict, Bryant Gumbel asked Willie Williams, soon to become L.A. Chief of Police, if he thought race played any part in the King jury's verdict.

Williams said, "I think race, to a certain degree, is part of everything we do in America, regardless of ethnicity."

Ken Burns, the brilliant documentary producer who gave us *The Civil War* and who is currently working on a baseball documentary, came on the show and addressed the issue.

"Race," he said, "is the central question in American history.

How we deal with it, how we don't deal with it, how we distort it, whatever. It's at the core of the Civil War, of course, it's at the core of our founding, it's at the core of baseball, and the parallel drama in the history of baseball is the story of race, and I think that's what needs to be told. We're not taking anything away from the joyous achievements of a game which is truly the national pastime."

I don't always agree with Spike Lee, but I loved Spike's Nike TV commercial where the white kids say, "I ain't playin' ball with no ball-hoggin', trash-talkin', showboatin', Nike-wearin', high-flyin', donut-dunkin', hip-hoppin' homeboy from Harlem."

And the black kids say, "And I ain't playin' ball with no flat-footed, Boston lovin', gravity-bound, Nike-wearin', no-dribblin', golden-haired hockey-playin' homeboy from South Dakota."

That's an amazing commercial, because those are common feelings out on the playgrounds, but we can't talk about them in polite company. Which is why Spike trotted them out. They have shock value, and shock creates action.

Ironically, Spike once took some hard shots on my show at the "white supremist" Boston Celtics, conveniently forgetting the Celtics' preeminent role in the integration of pro basketball.

Still, I agree with Spike that it's best to bring this stuff out, air it in public, in broad daylight, in mixed company. On TV. Get people riled up. Make them think and react.

We've done more shows on race-related issues than on any other topic, by far. To me it's not only vitally important, but endlessly fascinating. How do we come to grips with who we are? How do we interact? How does the struggle play itself out in sports?

I understand why many people feel race is not a burning issue, that all the frontiers have been crossed. It's a matter of isolation: see no evil.

With my stand-up act, I appear at fifty to sixty major corporate gatherings every year. I do not see black people in these audiences of America's power elite.

I'll go three or four appearances in a row without seeing a black face in the audience—or brown, or Asian, or female (except wives). The conclusion is obvious—America is very white at the top.

If this is your world, and then you sail off to your island of sports, watch Barry Bonds play for six million dollars a year and see black players dominating football and basketball, it's easy to think of America as a racial paradise. Jackie Robinson was a thousand years ago, now everything's cool.

We use sports to help us feel good about ourselves, to relieve our guilt. We look at Charles Barkley and Warren Moon raking in all that money and fame, and we expand those few cases to include thirty million blacks.

But as Barkley said, "Just because I'm doing well doesn't mean everybody is doing well."

Half of the white people in the country, according to a University of Chicago study, think black Americans are less patriotic, less courageous, less intelligent, and lazier than white people. If sports fans are a typical slice of Americana, half the white sports fans in the country (and half the general managers, and team owners) hold beliefs that would foster racial discrimination and tension.

Sport perpetuates the lies and distorts the images and puts us in a false comfort zone. Now and then we need be be jarred out. Not that I'm saving humanity on my little half hour on the tube. But if we can't look for human compassion and interaction, get people to express their feelings, it's all just balls and strikes on Fun Island.

Charlie Sifford is the only active athlete in America who goes back to the actual slave days of sport. He is a golfer, or that's what he has always tried to be—that and nothing more.

Sifford was thirty-six years old before he was allowed to play an occasional tournament on the white man's PGA tour. He was thirty-nine in 1961 when the PGA reluctantly scratched off the clause in its charter proclaiming that PGA tournaments are for "professional golfers of the Caucasian race." In 1961, Jackie Robinson had been *retired* from baseball five years.

Sifford turned seventy years old in 1992, and now competes on the Senior PGA Tour. He is a short, round gentleman who is never without his trademark cigar, even in the heat of tournament play. But Charlie is no clown. He is as serious an athlete as you'll find, and as angry.

When Charlie started wedging his foot in the door at PGA

tournaments, his caddy had to walk ahead to watch Sifford's shots land, and stand guard. Folks in the gallery had a habit of kicking Charlie's golf ball into the rough, or stacking bottles and cans around it.

In 1986 he played in a Los Angeles tournament in which anyone shooting a hole-in-one on a designated hole would win $100,000 and a new car. Charlie shot a hole-in-one. Oops! The sponsorship deal had fallen through, but somebody forgot to remove the sign at the hole. Sifford sued and won the $100,000, less about $30,000 in legal expenses.

Most guys would have chalked up the snafu to bad luck or human error. But if you've seen what Charlie's seen, you might have your suspicions.

"We black golfers haven't been pioneers as far as our sport is concerned," Charlie wrote in his autobiography. "We've been a few oddballs who somehow slipped through the cracks and were grudgingly allowed to play the game, in hopes that we'd just disappear under the pressures of the game and the tour."

I asked Sifford to explain the title of his book, *Just Let Me Play.*

"It really means that I didn't want anybody to get me anything," Sifford said. "All I wanted was the chance to play golf and prove to the world that a black man could play golf as well as a white man."

Charlie started as a caddy at an all-white club in North Carolina when he was thirteen. He was doing well, earning good money, learning the game. Then he got into an altercation with a local liquor store owner who called Charlie the N-word. A fight ensued, Charlie got the best of it, but also got tossed in jail.

"The guy I used to work for at the golf course was a wonderful man. His name was Sutton Alexander, and he owned the golf course, he's the one that let me play anytime he went out to play. But I used to sneak on the course and play, and a lot of the members would holler about it. When he found out that I was in jail, he came and bailed me out. He felt that I had a good chance to be a professional golfer."

But not in Charlotte. Sifford, still a teenager, moved to Philadelphia to pursue his golf dream. Even when the door finally started to open, it creaked. When he played in the Phoenix Open, Charlie couldn't get a hotel room, he wasn't allowed in the clubhouse, and when he pulled the pin at one hole (no caddies), he found a pile of human excrement.

"If I had been a bitter man, I never would have got as far as I've gotten," he said. "Those things I knew was going to happen if we continued to try to intercede in this game. Because first of all, it's tough, and second of all, they didn't want us in the game.

"I'm not trying to do anything to destroy the game of golf, but there's some things that should be a little better. They do have players that walk by you that won't speak to you. A lot of players, you understand, actually don't want you out there."

At the 1969 Los Angeles Open, California Attorney General Stanley Moss had to make legal threats to get Sifford into the tourney. Charlie won it.

"Moss called (the tournament officials) and told them that there was a man he wanted to enter, named Charles Sifford, so they said, 'He can't play,' and he said, 'Why?' and they said, 'He's not a member of the PGA.'

Never mind that the PGA wouldn't let Charlie join.

"Joe Louis is the one responsible for us getting into the tournament in Phoenix," Charlie said. "They wanted Joe to play, but he said he wouldn't play unless they had four black pros. That was Billy Spiller, Teddy Rhodes, Joe Roach, and myself."

Jackie Robinson wrote a commentary in the New York *Post* in support of Sifford's right to play golf.

"Jackie and I used to play out on Western Avenue (an L.A. course) all the time, and I told him what I was trying to do, and asked him what does he think about it. And he said, 'Well, I'll tell you, there's a lot of things you're going to run into. Are you a quitter?' And I said, 'No, I'm not a quitter.' And he said, 'Go ahead, but there's going to be some things in this game that are going to make you want to quit, so if you're going to quit, don't bother with it.' "

Sifford told an interesting story about Gary Player, the South African golfer who has been the target of anti-apartheid demonstrations. Sifford worked at a club in Cleveland years ago and was trying to build a reputation. One day he phoned Player, whose offices were in Cleveland, and asked him if he might give a clinic at Charlie's club.

Player gave a clinic for 750 club members, made Charlie look like a hero, then refused to accept any payment from Sifford.

"He said, 'Listen, laddie, not only do you not owe me anything, but keep on being a gentleman and do what you're doing and you'll be successful.' "

During a commercial break, Charlie told me that rather than mellowing with age, he was going in the opposite direction. In the old days he humbled himself because he needed the job. Now he vows to speak out, regardless of how it might affect his career.

I asked Charlie if he thought the racial situation in golf was ever going to get better.

"No," he said, "I don't think so."

It's like the phrase, "The battle is over, but the war goes on."

When the Shoal Creek controversy erupted in 1990, when it was exposed that many PGA Tour events are held at golf clubs that have racially exclusionary membership policies and/or practices, not one single pro golfer raised the slightest howl against this system, or expressed the slightest support or sympathy for the excluded minorities.

Except for one guy. Mac O'Grady. On our show.

O'Grady is considered by some to be a lunatic. He is considered by PGA Tour commissioner Deane Beman to be the loosest of loose cannons, but he was the only pro golfer even remotely bothered by the fact that his sport was revealed as blatantly insensitive to the widespread discrimination in America's country clubs.

"There's a certain socio-economic barrier here, that the black community cannot afford certain memberships," O'Grady said, "but in the long term, say over the last ten or fifteen years, the PGA Tour been practicing discrimination."

So you think they're lying when they say they had no knowledge of the Shoal Creek situation?

"Oh, absolutely."

O'Grady sarcastically described Beman as "our messiah."

"They're changing their policies right now because of the events of Shoal Creek," O'Grady said, "and the question is, in the past, the pure intent of it, why did not Beman change the policies six months ago or two years ago?"

O'Grady went on to say that "the players literally have an economic and social and political muzzle placed on them by Beman. He has conditioned these players, it doesn't matter who they are, even Nicklaus, Palmer, Tom Watson, are severely, severely scared of this man.

"If he is the game of golf and he is paid to administrate this tour, why wasn't this issue brought to light before?"

O'Grady, who obviously does not subscribe to the sport-as-island concept, said, "The game of golf itself is good because it teaches you about discipline and concentration and skills, and hopefully a little bit about spirituality and your love for your fellow man."

The greatest freedom fighter I've met is Father Thomas James, who is fighting a decidedly uphill battle.

By the end of this century, studies indicate, 70 percent of black men between the ages of eighteen and thirty-five will wind up in jail, on drugs, unemployed, or dead.

What can be done? A lot of it, I would guess, has to do with the educational system, and with people like Father James, who is the former headmaster at Verbum Dei High School in South Central Los Angeles.

A few years ago I wanted to find a black educator who was angry about the state of education and athletics, and Father James was the man. Verbum Dei is a very small Catholic high school, all boys. The students wear uniforms, and they all study and learn. Some play sports. Roy Hamilton, David Greenwood, Kenny Fields, and Vernon Maxwell are Verbum Dei grads.

In a section of the city where 80 percent of the kids don't finish high school, 80 percent of Verbum Dei students graduate and go on to earn college degrees.

What Father James and his school did/does is help kids escape what James calls "the ghetto of the mind," a deprivation of the soul, a failure to believe in oneself.

"When has the media done a story on the valedictorian at Manual Arts [an inner city high school in Los Angeles]?" Father James asked. "Who is talking about a black guy doing medical research at Drew University, on sickle-cell anemia? Nobody. Research is tedious. It's not clear-cut. We see a Kareem Abdul-Jabbar. We see an agent talking about two million dollars. That's impressive.

"But if all I can do is hit a ball, I am very limited as a person. I never develop my personhood. I become like a robot. Economic power, intellectual power, happens in the classroom."

Father James believes in sports, but as only one part of the educational process. When sport rules all one's being, he believes it to be a form of slavery. For many in the ghetto, success is thought of only in terms of accomplishment in sports or entertainment, and that thinking perpetuates itself, and it limits goals and dreams. It leads to many kids chasing completely unrealistic and unachievable goals.

"Sports is a means to an end," he says, "not the other way around. And it's been distorted by this nation, specifically the black community. It has cost us a great price, caused us to lose our direction as a people."

A crazy, sad fact of sports life is that, for all the Arthur Ashes and Father Jameses, the people who seem to wake people up to the injustices in sports are racially insensitive white leaders with foot-in-mouth disease.

Old Hall Thompson blew the lid off Shoal Creek CC and American golf. Al Campanis got baseball off its duff on the front-office hiring of minorities, although baseball settled right back onto its duff when the smoke cleared. When Marge Schott came along years later to wake us up again, we learned that baseball hadn't changed much, colorwise, as a result of Campanisgate.

What was sad about those incidents was that they provoked an outpouring of smug self-righteousness among most of us, and maybe not much else. Here we are, asleep at the wheel, crashing into a tree and praising ourselves for our sudden alertness.

Yes, Campanis and Thompson and Schott, and Jimmy "the Greek" Snyder to a lesser extent, deserved to be roasted, then let's move on to solve the problems that they point out.

They teach us a great lesson. Their foolishness reflects the worst aspects of the system—the lies, the ignorance, the inability to articulate fears. We should have spent less time talking about what was said and more about why these people felt as they did, where it was coming from. And what we could do to see that this thinking didn't carry over into action.

Campanis gets exiled from baseball in disgrace for a few words while Dodger owner Peter O'Malley comes off as the hero for booting Campanis. Where was O'Malley all those years when Campanis was, in a very nice and fatherly way, not hiring blacks to significant jobs?

Thompson becomes a national villain, while Beman and the PGA golfers, who have supported the golfing apartheid system by their participation and their silence, even after Thompson's confession, come off as innocent bystanders. As O'Grady said, "Hey Deane, where you been?"

Schott took the heat while the other owners, some of them with minority-hiring records as poor as hers, mopped their brows and went back into hiding.

Campanis, Snyder, Thompson, Schott—they are not the real threats to society. The real threats are the people who use them for lightning rods, use them to insulate themselves.

And those of us in the media, myself included, who should have been uncovering these racist practices, suddenly act like that's what we've done. But we learn from mistakes, and I do like to think that on the show we're trying to keep open the lines of dialogue and discussion, trying to throw the occasional beam of light into dark corners.

In 1991 I was given the Northeastern University School of Journalism Center for the Study of Sports and Society's annual award for excellence in sports journalism. One feeling I took away from that gathering in Boston was that unless the pressure is applied constantly by athletes, by activists, by journalists and others with a forum, progress is never going to be made. Voices have to speak out. Walter Payton saying we need black NFL owners. Henry Aaron pushing for more black involvement in baseball management.

I honestly believe that the all-white NFL coaching club was

finally broken up because media pressure, mainly from sportswriters, made the situation increasingly embarrassing to the NFL owners and commissioner.

That Northeastern award means so much to me, because—at the risk of sounding like Howard Cosell—the people at the Center honored our TV show for using interviews to apply pressure, to shed light, to be more than just talk, to be almost an advocacy.

In my acceptance speech I said I had ambivalent feelings. I said I felt the show did as much to trivialize sport as to elevate it. But sometimes tiny truths break through.

It's nice to uncover nuggets of insight, qualities in people that make it illuminating to spend ten minutes in conversation with them, maybe help someone watching to see they're not alone, that they have it within themselves all the time.

Of the players from baseball's Negro Leagues of the Thirties and Forties, only about 140 are still living, and many of them have sad stories. Many are broke, in bad physical shape, with no pensions or benefits from baseball.

Two former Negro League stars were on the show in 1992 to promote their International Organization of Athletes, a shoestring group that provides financial assistance to destitute Negro League veterans.

When Ban Johnson was baseball commissioner, he brushed off the Negro Leagues, saying, "They're not organized." To which one Negro Leaguer replied, "We're organized, we're just not recognized." Same today.

Sammie Haynes, former pitcher and coach, was one of the guests. He is in his late seventies and has been blind since 1965. He and Ray Welmaker talked about the old days, about surviving on two dollars a week meal money, sometimes playing three and four games a day, riding old buses through the deep South, hanging their soggy uniforms out the windows to dry on the fly, staying in fourth-rate motels and sharing bath water when they could get it.

I asked Sammie, "What's harder in life—poverty or loneliness?"

Sammie said, "You know what? I think poverty is harder, 'cause if you're lonely and you got a little bit of money, you can take a taxi and get somewhere and feel good."

I asked him if he felt resentful that the players were denied so much back then and continue to be snubbed by lack of pensions and assistance from "organized" baseball.

Sammie said, basically, that there's no room in his heart for hate.

Then he took a pin off his lapel and handed it to me.

"Tell me what this say, Roy."

It was black, white, red, yellow, and brown, with a heart in the middle, but no words.

"What it say there," Sammie said, "is all the colors have to be together. In the middle it say, 'It takes love.' "

Sammie thanked me for the times we had spoken out against racism on *Up Close*. For the first time ever on TV, I got a little choked up.

Here was a guy who had every reason to be angry and bitter, and he was talking about love. A small moment, but when we can talk about the human family, survival and dignity, and provide occasional moments of enlightenment, to me that outweighs a sack of letters from guys telling me, Enough's enough with the race stuff.

FOURTEEN

QUIET HEROES

"**S**how me a hero," F. Scott Fitzgerald said, "and I will write you a tragedy."

Show me a tragedy, I say, and I will show you a hero.

"Hero," I should emphasize, can be a touchy label. It conjures up the image of a person standing in the spotlight, being honored for courage above and beyond the call of duty.

Most of the heroes I've encountered don't want anything to do with being acclaimed for their heroism. But part of being a hero is not knowing you are one.

Let's just say that people I see as heroes are those who have been tested in circumstances that seem crushingly difficult to me, and have dealt with the hand given them in ways that I find courageous and inspiring.

I should call them "people whom I admire," but "heroes" sounds cooler, and, after all, it's my book.

Tom Sullivan is a great friend and a great guest, and a quiet hero who is seldom quiet.

Even though he's not a pro athlete, Tom is a valuable asset to me as a sports observer because he sees the games better than just about anybody I know.

Although he doesn't see in the commonly accepted sense, having been blind since birth, Tom misses nothing.

He is a major Laker fan, has season tickets right behind Jack Nicholson.

"When you listen to a game," Sullivan tells me, "you can learn anything about it—how the players are moving, the patterns on the floor.

"You can tell if they're getting back on defense by the squeak of their shoes. You listen for foul shots that hit the rim like a rock. I sit behind the visitors' bench and I love it when teams come to the sidelines for timeouts because I can hear everything that's going on in there.

"And I can absolutely know in the third quarter where a team is coming from by what the coach is saying, and by whether his players are paying attention, and I can tell that by the tightness of their circle. Is everybody's voice coming from the same place?"

Tom says Magic Johnson had the most distinctive dribble in basketball.

"His dribble makes you know he is surveying the floor. It's slow, as if, in his head, he had all day. Kareem had the same approach—'I'll shoot this when I'm ready.'

"I can tell who caught a pass. [James] Worthy is the only player in the league who always catches the pass one-handed. Always in his right hand, you never hear the second hand close on the ball.

"I can tell which referee blew the whistle. Earl Strom had a whistle that's real quick, like, 'It's my court, you only play here.' Strom was the voice of authority. He only blew his whistle once. Whereas Jake O'Donnell is very much an elegant referee. The whistle is long. Joey Crawford blows several toots, you think he's going to hyperventilate."

Fascinating stuff, but what's even more interesting about Sullivan is certain elemental truths he has discovered, which apply to athletes and to all of us.

By the way, Tom is a creative whirlwind, lives life with a vengeance. He has written five books, including a current bestseller, *The Leading Lady.* He plays piano, sings, and composes, and has recorded five albums, three of which made the top twenty. He has been a TV interviewer, and is a TV actor, motivational speaker, movie producer, major charity fundraiser, husband, philosopher, avid recreational athlete, sports fan . . . and I'm sure he does a lot of interesting things in his spare time.

Tom's philosophy is "You need to appreciate beauty, obey instincts, be spontaneous, and achieve balance."

We've been friends since the first time he came on the show, in 1986, promoting his charity ten-kilometer run. Tom and I hit it off immediately.

He is my toughest critic. Sullivan and my wife, Midori, are my Siskel and Ebert. Tom will call me after a bad show and say sarcastically, "I saw the show last night. I could tell you were really into it."

He'll also tell me when I seemed particularly moved or inspired by a guest. Tom's not distracted by the flashiness of TV, so he is the best ear I have, and the best eye.

He understands sports because he understands so well the meaning and the application of competitive anger, which has accounted for his ambition and success, and for that of probably every great athlete.

As a boy Tom went to a school for the blind, where he excelled in everything—sports, academics, music. He would go home on weekends and he would suddenly be the blind kid on the block.

He says, "I remember thinking, 'If I'm the best among the blind, and the worst among the sighted, where is my place?' "

He had to find that place, and it was not easy.

"Frankly, Roy, loneliness was the big motivator," he said. "I was a little boy in Boston, in a backyard with a high fence. My dad put up the fence; the idea was to keep the world outside and let the handicapped child stay in. It was safe.

"Down the street there was a ball field. I can remember the ballgame going on, the sound of the bat hitting the ball, the sound of the ball popping into people's gloves, and I wanted to play.

"So I picked up a stick and a rock. Every time a little boy would hit the baseball with his bat, I would hit a rock with my stick. Well, this little kid from the game came by the fence one day and he looked through the wire and he said, 'Howya doin', Blindy?'

"Now he didn't mean any harm. He was responding to his sense of my label. But what happened in that moment is exactly what needs to happen to every kid in every ghetto in this country. I became competitively angry. I said to myself, 'Wait, I *am* lonely, I *am* hurt, and I've got to make a decision right now, at seven years old, that I am not going to stay inside this fence.'

"And I think every human in this country has to do that, I think we are all disabled. Some of us are shy, some of us are growing older and we're upset about it. Some of us are too heavy, some of us feel that we aren't cutting it in our jobs, some of us put so much time into our jobs we're not making it happen in our marriages. But those are disabilities, and you either turn disadvantages into advantages, or fold up.

"There has never been a successful person that didn't have competitive anger driving their natural talents to the surface."

Young Tom decided that he would play ball with the other kids. His dad put up a basketball goal over the driveway and hung a transistor radio just under the rim. Tom would aim for the music. When the radio took a beating, his dad put up a buzzer, which drove the neighbors crazy.

Tom would challenge the other kids to free-throw–shooting contests, and he found that if he waited until dark, his opponents would have a distinct handicap.

He loved sports and had a vivid imagination.

"What I'd do, I'd find a sports station and turn on an announcer, and if it was football, I'd take a football out there and as the play happened I'd throw myself down on the ground. Or I'd throw the ball against the fence like a forward pass. Or if it was baseball, I'd hit a rock with a stick.

"If it was basketball, when [announcer] Johnny Most was talking about the Celtics, I was shooting the shots at my buzzer.

"If I could make myself believe I could play, then when I entered neighborhood life with sighted children, I believed I could. Until they burst my bubble."

And what was that like?

"Oh, boy. You know me too well, Roy. Well, you know when you're a kid and you're in the yard or neighborhood, and sides are picked? And you'd pick captains and they'd start selecting their teams? 'I'll take Jim.' 'I'll take Johnny.'

"So the teams would get chosen up and I was the last one, and there'd be a pause, and a little boy would say, 'I'll take *him.*' They never said my name. 'I'll take *him.*'

"What saved me was competitive anger. I wanted so much to be loved and involved that I competed to get that. I'm convinced as an adult that what we need in life most of all is passion. There's no casual way to carry on a life process and be a winner. You have to have passion."

Tom's handicap, naturally, has limited his athletic endeavors as an adult. All he does is water ski, snow ski, run, bungee jump, and golf, and he was a wrestler in college.

Stevie Wonder coined a phrase—Inner Vision. That's Tom.

A few years after Bob "Butterbean" Love retired from basketball, from a brilliant career as one of the great forwards of his era, he was working as a busboy in a Seattle restaurant.

A riches-to-dishrags story.

This was the same Butterbean Love whom Bill Bradley, a fellow NBA forward and a Rhodes Scholar, once referred to as the smartest man in the NBA.

But Love had a severe stutter. He tried speech therapy several times through the years, but mostly it consisted of reading books aloud and talking to strangers, and it never worked. That was okay, because Love could think just fine, and he could play ball.

"No one felt sorry for him," said Chet Walker, a former Bulls teammate. "He was funny, a riot in card games, never stuttered then, or when he would cuss."

He played for the Bulls and two other teams, eleven seasons, had a 17.6 lifetime scoring average. At 6' 8" and 215 pounds, he was fast, agile and graceful.

He got along with his teammates, and made pretty good money. When Dick Motta coached the Bulls, Love missed practice one day, phoning in that his car wouldn't start.

"Must be an epidemic," Motta mused. "Bob's got five cars."

Love lived well and played well. In 1977 a bad back forced him to retire a little sooner than he expected to. He was thirty-four and had most of his life in front of him. In this same situation, many athletes ease into a cushy postcareer life of PR work or sales, some form of exploiting their name and fame.

But Bob was severely limited by his stuttering. Basketball work was out of the question. Any kind of front-office or scouting or coaching job involves talking. Radio and TV work? Not a prayer.

When he went looking for jobs, it was almost as if he were retarded. He couldn't communicate, he couldn't even look people in the eye because his severe stutter caused him to make facial contortions and he was deeply self-conscious. Cold reality set in. He ran out of luck and dropped out of sight.

Twelve years later, in 1989, I hosted the NBA Player Awards at the Chicago Marriott. Bob Love was there to receive a Lifetime Achievement Award. When the presentation was made he stepped up to the microphone and began to speak to the one thousand guests.

"Please understand that this is a new experience for me, and it's a little scary," he said.

He spoke for ten minutes, slowly and a bit haltingly, but eloquently, about what it is to be a man, to have courage and believe in yourself, to deal with life.

He received a standing ovation. Many in the audience were in tears. Not long after that he came on the show and told his story.

"People tend to think that if you have a speech handicap, something is wrong with you mentally," he said. "I was just struggling to find myself. I had just had my second back operation, I didn't really have a job, I didn't know if I would ever walk right again.

"In 1983 I was married, but the person I was married to left me and basically took everything I had. Economically, it practically destroyed me because I was unable to make any outside income."

In 1984, desperate, Love took a job as a busboy in the kitchen of the Nordstrom department store in downtown Seattle.

"A lot of my friends would come into the cafe and they would say, 'That's Bob Love there. He used to be a great, great basketball player, but now he's busing tables.'

"You know what I did? I took that opportunity to show them

that I was a man. I became the best busser in the world, and I'm not ashamed that I did it."

Soon he was promoted, to dishwasher. Then to food-prep cook. Then he was assigned to work the cash register. In the spring of 1986 he started seeing a speech therapist.

"My problem, I grew up down South in a little town called Bastrop, Louisiana, and during the time I was growing up we didn't have no idea about speech therapy. My grandmother would try to do a lot of things, like hittin' me in the mouth with a dish rag.

"I used to dream of myself standin' in front of thousands of people, telling them about my life and what I did. I would have their attention for thirty minutes or an hour. Despite the fact I had these problems, I kept that dream alive for forty-five years, I never gave up on it."

The therapy started working. Love turned his life around, over-came his fears, got promoted up and up the ladder, gaining confidence. He is now the Nordstrom Corporate Director of Health. He gives speeches all over the Northwest, telling his story, talking about self-worth and self-image, spreading hope and inspiration.

And now Bob Love can hardly remember way back when he thought basketball was the way he would make his name and his impact on people.

It's tempting to wrap people's lives in neat packages. When someone like a Bob Love is on the program, or a Dave Dravecky, it's nice to close out the show by explaining how this person, who has gone through so much and overcome so much, is now living happily ever after.

That's never the truth, of course. I've learned that you take a person for what he is at the moment, be it a moment on our show or a moment beyond the camera. You never say, "There you have it, ladies and gentlemen—an inspiring case study of a guy who beat the system."

Walter Davis was on the show and he talked about how drugs ruined his life, cost him his marriage, but through rehabilitation he found himself and became a whole person.

It was a very moving interview, a strong human statement. Two days after we taped the show, Davis checked himself into a drug rehab center.

I got a couple calls from people saying, "Don't you feel betrayed by Davis? He came on your show and lied, made you look foolish."

Ridiculous. What Walter said and felt on the show was real. The fact that he had some trouble living up to his dreams and ideals doesn't make him a liar, it makes him a human.

Dave Dravecky came on the show after his left arm, his pitching arm, had been amputated. He had gone through so much, fighting the cancer, coming back to baseball, then having his pitching arm literally snap when he threw a pitch, and then the amputation, and the adjustment.

It was tempting for me to hold him up as a guy who had conquered, who has planted the flag at the top of the mountain. In reality, no matter how noble the climb, the summit can never be reached.

Nobody's life, at any point, is a neat little package.

Dravecky still had the pain and fears and anxieties and insecurities that go with living with cancer, and with simply being alive. In some ways this walking metaphor for courage was scared to death.

I found Dravecky inspiring because he wasn't afraid to let us know that everything is not okay, that you can face the world bravely and positively, but the battle goes on.

He talked about a crisis of confidence that came when he was on a speaking tour, preaching a spiritual message of hope and courage.

"I decided in the midst of the tour that I didn't know if I wanted to speak to people anymore," Dravecky said. "I was in California, I was on a five-day trip, speaking at five different places to about ten thousand people and signing thousands of autographs.

"I came home after that trip and I laid down in my bed, and I'll never forget this because I was there with Jan (his wife), and she looked at me and wanted to know what was wrong. And I said, 'I've had it. I just want to stop all of this and chuck it in, because I don't feel like doing it any more.'

"People say, 'Wow, what a courageous guy,' and you want to be buoyed by all the public support, but you still have to come to a reckoning with this [the arm], or the lack of this.

"In a certain sense you're almost being asborbed by all the public adulation. It was keeping you a distance from the reality. A lot of it was a form of Dave being able to deny what was really going on with him. One of the biggest problems I had when I left the hospital from the amputation was that I left on such a high, because I was ready to accept what happened and move forward with my life.

"And as I went through that period of time for the first few months, I was feeding off of all these people that I was going to speak to, and I was being blessed as much as I was blessing, and that helped me to deal with what I was going through, and in reality what I did was I suppressed it, I pushed it down.

"I've always been able to succeed, I was invincible, and when you come out of that realm and you know for the first time you can't change the situation you're in, you realize how much you need others.

"I'm at that point now, I'm reaching out to other people, really seeking those relationships that can help me as I go through this."

Dravecky talked about a letter he received from an inmate on death row at San Quentin.

"He had become a Christian in prison and was a part of the prison ministry. He said he recognized his punishment, but this letter meant so much because it showed me what it means to truly have a servant's heart. He offered me his humerus bone. I started reading the letter and got halfway through the first page and couldn't finish. I was in tears, it just meant so much to me."

I asked Dravecky about the cloud that forever hangs over his head, the cancer.

"I struggle a great deal with that. I didn't let anyone know it, but the reality is that I was scared. I was afraid when I thought about my children, and someone else being their father, and my wife and someone else being her husband, and I didn't like that feeling at all, I didn't like those thoughts.

"And one of the things that helped me to deal with that was to not take for granted the special gifts that they are to me. And in the process I spent more time, and now I don't worry about the little things, the arguing and bickering. I try to make the most of every day."

He continued, saying that he was glad to be a voice for other people who are struggling with cancer or being an amputee. He decided to choose to see what good could come out of this, and to see how he could help others and be helped in turn.

Dravecky helped publicize one particular young boy's need for a compatible bone-marrow transplant donor, and seven thousand volunteers answered the call.

"He has been such an inspiration to me," Dravecky said of the boy. "It's amazing to see the spirit in him, and the determination. And this is going to help not only him, but by adding seven thousand names to the donor registry, it increases the chances of others to have an opportunity to live."

Does any of what has happened to you ever cause you to reflect on how cruel God can be?

"When I think about the valuable lesson I've learned as I've gone through this process, I feel like what God has done is take me and actually shape and mold me into something even better than I was before."

But no matter how inspiring his story, Dravecky is, and always will be, a work in progress.

When Frank Deford and his wife Carol lost a seven-year-old daughter to cystic fibrosis, Frank did the only thing he could do. He sat down and wrote his heart out, spilled words like tears.

Alex: The Life of a Child was Deford's way of mourning, and of celebrating a life that ended too soon, and of sharing the grief and the love and what he had felt and learned.

Frank came on the show and talked about how he owed it to Alex not only to carry on, but to find a higher meaning from this personal tragedy. He has, for instance, served as national chairman of the Cystic Fibrosis Foundation, and he and Carol adopted a daughter, Scarlet, from the Philippines. And Frank wrote the book.

Frank is America's sportswriter, a legend at *Sports Illustrated*

for years, a novelist *(Everybody's All-American),* and a TV personality. When Alex died, her father kept on writing.

"If I had let her death destroy me, that would have been the
worst thing that I could have done to her," Deford said. "She felt
bad enough about dying without having us die inside. It's good to
have a guardian angel. I'd rather have *her* around, but if I can't
have her around, it's nice to have a guardian angel."

He said that writing the book was easy, because the love simply
poured out. The book-promotion tour was a different matter.
Naturally he wanted people to read the book, he wanted to share,
but the selling of it was tough.

I asked him if talking about Alex reopened old wounds.

"I don't know if reopen is the word, since those wounds have
never gone away. It's certainly made those wounds deeper. But
you know, there's another thing about it, Roy, people sometimes
forget this—I loved Alex very much and this gives me a natural
excuse to think about her and to talk about her. You can't dwell
on death, and you can't hang on artificially to people who have
long since gone, but I've got an excuse to do it, and in that sense
it's very nice."

*The doctor who diagnosed Alex told you your child would give
you a great deal of joy and love. You were frightened by the fact
that you would grow to know Alex.*

"I am not a saint, I am the father of a saint. People are always
saying, 'Oh, how wonderful you are,' and I say, 'Wait, slow down,
I just wrote the book.' "

*Is there a lot of guilt because you felt like you could never be
as good as Alex?*

"Still feel that way, still feel that if suddenly I found myself in
a life-threatening situation, that I would never handle it nearly as
well as a seven-year-old child did. That frightens me.

"By the same token, maybe it's going to force me, if I find
myself in that situation, to say to myself, 'Come on, now, you owe
it to Alex to at least do almost as good as she did."

*You wrote, ''More fury is growing within me that Alex never
had a fair chance.''*

"I suppose that's been muted by time. I've gone on to other

things, and I'm using Alex now for very good reasons, which she would have delighted in, if she'd known she would become a personification of children with cystic fibrosis. She's given us an opportunity to let more people know about cystic fibrosis. Just sitting here talking to you, for example.

"And so I've tried to replace a negative response as much as possible with a positive one. But I'd be lying to you if I didn't say that I'm still mad she's not here. She'd be fourteen years old now, and I'd love to see Alex be fourteen."

Someone once said, ''You have to learn to make friends with death.''

"That's a curious turn of phrase. I don't know if I would use the affection angle. But I do think that you would have to learn to deal with death, I think we all do.

"It's a little more difficult for children because a child has never been anywhere alone. Suddenly, on top of everything else, you're not only going to die, but you have to go off by yourself. Alex was very concerned, as are all terminally ill children, about being left alone there on the last days of her life.

"Yes, she was worried about dying herself, but she made a classic remark to the nurse when she left the hospital for the last time: 'I'm going home to die, but don't tell my mommy and daddy, because it would upset them.'

"And she had a brother, Chris, who's now sixteen, and she was particularly worried about him, because, as she pointed out, her mother and I still have each other, we weren't losing a mate, but Chris was losing his only sibling. She was worried about him terribly."

In 1972 you sat down and wrote a letter to Alex while she was still alive.

"This was shortly after she had been diagnosed and given up for dead, and then a week later they said, 'It looks like she's going to make it.' My wife was still with her in Boston and I came back to work in Connecticut, and I was alone one night with the dog, and this is what I wrote to Alex:

" 'If I could pray for one thing in my life, it is that you will be back here soon, before spring comes, and then you will grow up here with us, and you will grow up smart, and clever, and pretty, and happy, and strong and healthy, too. You must see spring, Alex, the next spring and the one after, and each spring will find you better.

" 'And one best spring, when the cold goes away and the wind blows over the fresh green grass and the robins bring our dreams back, then you will be well. And then you and I will walk on clover, and peer through the dogwood back to 1972, and laugh together that ever I worried that you might not come home and grow up.' "

How do you look at life, in view of your tragedy?

"I view it—and this will strike you as odd—very pragmatically. People say, 'Weren't you cheated, isn't this awful? God played a mean trick on you.' You have to look at everything. God also put me in the United States of America, a white male, he gave me a talent, he gave me a family, the great love of parents and brothers and sisters.

"So if you're going to rail at the mean things that happen to you, you'd better also recognize and give thanks for the blessings."

When the delivery-room doctor told football coach Gene Stallings that his newborn son had Down's syndrome, Stallings wanted to punch the doctor in the face.

Stallings is a strong, tough man. Militaristic, a John Wayne-type. You don't deal with life, with problems—you attack. You take control. But here was a new and confusing situation, a human being who could not be whipped into shape like a lazy offensive lineman.

Instead, it is Gene who has been whipped into shape by John Mark Stallings—Johnny.

Gene came on the show shortly after he had been fired by the Phoenix Cardinals in 1989, and before he had hired on to coach the University of Alabama, and talked about his son.

Johnny, then twenty-six, had been the Cardinals' assistant equipment man when Gene was coach.

"Johnny has asked me several times, 'Pop, the Cardinals gonna hire you back?' And I say, 'No, Johnny, I don't really think so.' Drivin' up Sunday, we were listening to the ballgame, and when the Cardinals got behind he sort of got quiet, and he said, 'Pop, Hank's sad." [new coach Hank Kuhlmann], and I said, 'Yeah, probably is.' And he said, 'I love Hank,' and I said, 'Yeah, I know you do, Johnny.'

"We went a little bit further and he said, 'I bet Donna's sad, too.' Donna is Hank's wife. So Johnny is very sensitive. He said two or three times, 'Is [General manager] Larry Wilson your friend?' I said, 'Yeah, Johnny.' 'Is he gonna give you your job back?' I said, 'No, I don't think so.' "

It was a sad little vignette, of a young man with the mind of a small boy, wrestling with a father's setback and with upheaval in his own world.

But the way Stallings told the story, with warmth and love, it obviously was not a sad story. It was his way of describing the depth of feeling in his son, the love they have for one another. In fact Gene, who also has four daughters, is constantly amazed by the amount of love his son is capable of giving.

"Not only do I love him, I like him," Stallings said. "If you'd say, 'Johnny, why do you want the Cardinals to win?' He'll say, 'Because it makes Pop happy.' He's made me a more compassionate person. I feel for the second-team player, where I don't think I would have had that feeling."

The infinite variety of tragedy always amazes me. Personal tragedies are sort of like snowflakes, no two alike.

Lonise Bias, for example, has suffered a double tragedy of violent death. Her son, Len, was a power forward at Maryland, drafted in the first round by the Boston Celtics in 1986. He was twenty-two and he looked like the future of the Celtic franchise, Larry Bird's new partner in crime.

Two days later Len was dead of a cocaine overdose. He had no known drug-abuse history, but he had celebrated a great personal triumph in a foolish manner and it killed him.

Four years later, Lonise's second son, Jay, age twenty and also a ballplayer, got into a quarrel at a shopping mall in Maryland and was shot to death.

When the mother's grieving subsided, what was left was anger. Lonise Bias took the anger and went to war with it.

She has become a preacher of sorts, a person with a message which she delivers dozens of times a year on TV, in school assemblies, wherever people will listen to her sermon of warning and hope.

She is an example of Tom Sullivan's "competitive anger" at work, channeled into a productive—rather than self-destructive—rage.

"It's only when you're kicked out of your comfortable position that you maximize your potential," she said. "And in going through something very painful, I have grown and developed. I know when I do the type of programs that I'm doing, there are going to be memories from the past, but it does not necessarily bring up pain. I prefer to stay focused on where we're going and not looking back."

One of her themes is what might be called the misapplication of sports in America. She believes that in the USA, one of our greatest problems is not understanding that sports is only entertainment, not life.

"I believe that coaches must realize they're educators, and when children are taken from their parents' home, coaches have a responsibility to take care of that child to the best of their ability. We need coaches to keep showing the same type of enthusiasm they have when they come into your home to recruit your son.

"It's the system, and parents see how the system runs and they still send their children into the system. So parents must take a stand and say that we want the best for our child, the same type of quality time they put in on the court or on the field, we want it in the classroom as well."

Drug use is up, and fifteen thousand to twenty thousand young people commit suicide each year.

"We must understand that we as adults are the educators, and the children are confused. Confused adults cannot lead children. It is so hypocritical for us as adults to look at children and say that the children have problems, when you must look at the adults who have to chart a course for the children to take.

"We still have so many problems with substance abuse, primar ily because we continue to try to address substance abuse without addressing issues of immorality. We tell young people to say no to drugs and alcohol, but it's still okay to tell a lie, it's still okay to disrespect your parents. Drugs and alcohol are only a symptom, these children have deep emotional problems that need to be met.

"I am a firm believer that money and education and prosperity will not correct immorality. Education academically is fine, but we must also give the education of self-love."

How far down can you sink and still rise up and conquer?

Probably the ultimate answer to that question was provided at the 1992 Summer Olympics by Gail Devers. Only two years before, Devers had been reduced to crawling, literally, and praying that her feet would not have to be amputated.

She battled back from an extreme case of Graves' disease, and at Barcelona she made it to the semifinals of the 100 meters. She broke out of the blocks slowly, yet qualified for the finals.

"What's wrong?" asked Bob Kersee, Devers's coach.

"I can't feel my feet," Devers said.

Kersee told her, "This is the Olympic Games. You've worked hard to get here. If you can't feel your feet, you work your arms and tell your feet to keep up."

She did, and they did, and Devers won the gold medal. And narrowly missed another gold in the 100-meter hurdles, when she stumbled and finished fifth.

Devers was on the show just before leaving for the Olympics, and as courageous as her comeback had been, it seemed unlikely that she would become anything but an extremely inspiring participant at Barcelona.

Of all the injury and comeback stories in sport, I'm not sure I've heard a more terrifying one than she told us.

Late in 1988 she began to experience excruciating pains in her feet and paralyzing migraines. Several doctors misdiagnosed her, including one who told her she had a severe case of athlete's foot. Others chalked it up to stress, or fatigue.

Graves' disease causes the thyroid gland to fluctuate wildly between way too much output and way too little, creating a horrible yo-yo effect on weight and energy, with a carload of side effects.

How did you look two and a half years ago?

"In my opinion, like a creature. I used to call myself the alligator woman. My face was like when a snake starts to shed its skin—half of it's on, half of it's off. I stopped looking in a mirror. My eyes were bulging out. I'd always had large eyes, but this was ridiculous, where one was larger than the other, and they both protruded. You could see my skeleton because I'd lost so much weight, and it wasn't pleasant."

It affected your weight and sleep.

"I went from insomnia to comatose, where my body was actually in a coma. I would sleep sixteen hours a day, or be up for forty-eight hours, there was no middle ground. I had memory loss, hair loss. I am so thankful to have hair now.

"I had involuntary shakes, uncontrollable. My running weight was between 117 and 120, and I lost so much weight I wouldn't let anyone put me on a scale until I started gaining, and once I started gaining I was at 97 pounds. Quickly I zoomed up to 139 pounds. Within weeks."

The illness contributed to the breakup of her marriage, but close friends, such as Jackie Joyner-Kersee and Greg Foster, refused to let Devers give up, even when the symptoms got worse.

Your feet would swell up to two and three times their normal size, plus they would bleed. You couldn't work out. You were told to stay off your feet.

"I had blood blisters, lesions, holes in my feet oozing yellow fluid, causing a terrible stench. I couldn't wear shoes and when I'd take off my socks, I would pull off layers of skin."

Finally the problem was properly diagnosed, but further complications put Devers a week away from having both feet amputated, until she rallied. Devers said that she doubted herself after seeing three or four doctors. She began to think that perhaps she was just being a hypochondriac.

Why do you think you didn't quit? It would have been so easy just to completely give up.

"I definitely wanted to give up track and field. Before I was diagnosed, I thought it was just me, that I was washed up. And once I found out that it wasn't me, that I just happened to be plagued with a disease, it was like, 'Okay, Gail, you're fine, once you get this treatment under way, you're gonna be back to where you were.'"

You had to have your thyroid removed, and you will have to have hormones the rest of your life, and it's going to be difficult. Have you accepted the fact that your life is going to be changed?

"To me it's a small price to pay to be here. I'm actually thankful to have gone through my Graves' disease, now that I'm through it, because it's changed me as a person, made me stronger and more determined.

"And I would tell anybody, the last three years of my life is like a miracle. If you don't believe dreams come true, look at me. You have to have faith and believe in yourself."

By now, if I don't believe in dreams and miracles and the triumph of the human spirit, I haven't been paying attention.